THE ROYAL EDINBURGH MILITARY TATTOO

'The Show Must Go On'
Travels of The Tattoo Producer

Brigadier Sir Melville Jameson

To my wife Sarah and my family
For keeping the home fires burning

The Royal Edinburgh Military Tattoo © 2025.
All rights reserved.
The right of Melville Jameson to be identified as the author of
the Work has been asserted in accordance with the Copyright,
Designs & Patents Act 1988.
This first edition published and copyright 2025 by
Tippermuir Books Ltd, Perth, Scotland.
mail@tippermuirbooks.co.uk – tippermuirbooks.co.uk.

No part of this publication may be reproduced or used
in any form or by any means without written permission from
the Publisher except for review purposes.
All rights whatsoever in this book are reserved.

ISBN 978-1-913836-38-2 (paperback).

A CIP catalogue record for this book is available from
the British Library.

Project coordination and editorial by Paul S Philippou.
Cover design by Kate Osmond. Cover Photo by Mark Owen.
Editorial support: Steve Zajda and Jean Hands.
Co-founders and publishers of Tippermuir Books:
Rob Hands, Matthew Mackie and Paul S Philippou.

Text design, layout, and artwork by Bernard Chandler [graffik].
Text set in Bulmer Regular MT Std 11/14pt with Bulmer Semi Bold Italic titling.

Printed and bound by CPI Antony Rowe.
This book has been printed in the UK to reduce transportation miles
and their impact on the environment. It has been printed to comply
with the Forest Stewardship Council (FSC) Chain of Custody
requirements and paper sourcing from responsibly managed sources.

THE ROYAL EDINBURGH
MILITARY TATTOO

MELVILLE STEWART JAMESON was born and brought up at his home in Perthshire and educated at Glenalmond College. In 1965, he was commissioned into the Royal Scots Greys from The Royal Military Academy Sandhurst. He served with his regiment in Northern Ireland, Germany, Cyprus, the Middle East and Edinburgh, where in 1971 his regiment was amalgamated with the 3rd Carabiniers to form The Royal Scots Dragoon Guards.

He commanded his regiment between 1986 and 1988; on promotion to brigadier, he was appointed Commander 51 Highland Brigade based in Perth in 1993. In 1995, however, he was selected to be the producer of The Royal Edinburgh Military Tattoo, and, in 1997, he left the Army early to assume the official appointment of producer and chief executive.

On leaving The Royal Edinburgh Military Tattoo, he was appointed as Lord-Lieutenant of Perth and Kinross and at the end of his tenure of twelve years was granted a knighthood by HM The Queen (KCVO) and given the rare tribute of 'Freedom of the City' by the Provost and Councillors of Perth and Kinross. He is married to Sarah and has two sons: Harry, married to Frippy, and Michael, married to Hatti; and five grandchildren.

In 2007, he retired from The Tattoo but continued to act as a consultant for military musical events and tattoos across the world. He co-produced the first Kremlin Tattoo on Red Square in Moscow in 2007. He was the producer of The Royal Windsor Tattoo under the direction of The Royal Windsor Horse Show. Later, he was consultant producer for The Queen's Diamond Jubilee Pageant, Her Majesty's 90th Birthday celebrations and her Platinum Jubilee celebration. For many years, he was the senior adviser to The Royal Edinburgh Military Tattoo and is presently the senior adviser to The Basel Tattoo in Switzerland.

The book is the story of his time as producer/chief executive of The Royal Edinburgh Military Tattoo.

CONTENTS

Chapter One	1995	1
Chapter Two	1996	7
Chapter Three	1997	13
Chapter Four	1998	25
Chapter Five	1999	33
Chapter Six	2000	39
Chapter Seven	2001	49
Chapter Eight	2002	59
	Picture Gallery	*after page* 70
Chapter Nine	2003	71
Chapter Ten	2004	81
Chapter Eleven	2005	89
Chapter Twelve	2006	99
Chapter Thirteen	Post-Edinburgh	111
Appendix	'Amazing Grace' by The Royal Scots Dragoon Guards	127

LIST OF ILLUSTRATIONS

Many of the photographs in the book were taken by Mark Owen, The Tattoo Official Photographer who must be thanked for permission to use them.

HER ROYAL HIGHNESS THE PRINCESS ROYAL

Lieutenant Colonel Richard Hambleton, Financial Director and Steve Walsh, Production Manager (1995)

Cast Lunch at Easter Logie (1995)

Gazelle Helicopter Transporting Some of the 1995 Cast to Easter Logie for Lunch (1995)

The Pipes and Drums of the Egyptian Army (1995)

The Gate to the Khyber Pass (1996)

New Zealand Police Pipes and Drums Competing at Invercargill (1996)

Pipe Sergeant in the 8th Kashmir Regiment Pakistan (1996)

US Army Silent Drill Display Team (1996)

Highland Dancer (1997)

Menu for Lunch with Commander of the Fiji Defence Forces (1998)

Cook Islands Dancers (1998)

Barbados Army Band (1999)

Zulus From the Zulu Battalion (Mtubatuba Kwa Zulu), Natal (2000)

Adelaide Mounted Police (2000)

The Tattoo Performs in New Zealand – Massed Pipes and Drums (2000)

The Tattoo Performs in New Zealand – The Finale (2000)

Bermuda Gombey Dancers (2001)

The Bermuda Regiment Band (2001)

Cook Islands Dancers (2001)

Cossack Dancer (2001)

The Queen Meets the Cast of The Queen's Golden Jubilee Edinburgh Military Tattoo (2002)

The Queen's Golden Jubilee Edinburgh Military Tattoo [Painted by Douglas N Anderson] (2002)

Visit by The Queen to The Golden Jubilee Edinburgh Military Tattoo (2002)

Ramillies The Drum Horse of The Royal Scots Dragoon Guards and a Mounted Troop of The Life Guards (2002)

Mounted Troop From The Royal Scots Dragoon Guards with Ramillies the Drum Horse (2002)

The New Zealand Army Band (2002)

Police Guard of Honour at the Visit to the Governor of Manipur (2002)

Traditional Army Band of Korea (2003)

Royal Palace in Tonga (2003)

Visit to 61st Cavalry, Jaipur, India (2003)

Traditional Army Band of Korea Dancers (2003)

Traditional Army Band of Korea Dancers (2003)

Gombey Dancers From Bermuda (2003)

Traditional Dancers From the Royal Palace, Oman (2003)

The Princess Royal, Melville Jameson and the Lord Provost, Lesley Hinds (2003)

US Army Silent Drill Display Team (2003)

Top Secret Drum Corps (2003) – *Two pictures*

HRH The Princess Royal Talks to the Cast After The Tattoo (2003)

The Massed Pipes and Drums March on From The Drawbridge (2004)

Cheraw Dancers From India (2004)

The People's Liberation Army Display Team From China (2004)

The People's Liberation Army Band China (2004)

Club Piruett Gymnastic Team From Estonia (2004)

The Band of the South African Navy – Director of Music, Commander Mike Oldham Plays the Solo (2004)

The Royal Air Force Massed Bands Drum Major (2004)

Highland Dancers (2004)

Rowena Macrae – Solo Violinist at the Finale (2004)

The Massed Bands of The Royal Marines Celebrate The 200th Anniversary of the Battle of Trafalgar (2005)

The King's Guard of Norway (2005)

The Imps Motorcycle Display Team (2005)

The Finale (2005)

Trinidad and Tobago Steel Orchestra (2005)

Khattak Dancers From the Khyber Regiment Pakistan (2005)

The Finale of The Edinburgh Military Tattoo, Aussie Stadium, Sydney (2005)

The Massed Pipes and Drums Emerge From the Drawbridge (2005)
Kung Fu Display From China (2006)
Prince Edward, Earl of Wessex (2006)
Watoto Orphans Choir, Uganda (2006)
New Zealand Army Band (2006)
Army of Chile Concert Band With Melville Jameson (2006)
Argentinian Patricios Regimental Band (2006)
The Finale (2006)
The Royal Edinburgh Tattoo (2006)
Sean Connery Presenting Edinburgh Castle to Melville Jameson
  at his Farewell, Mel's ADC, Captain Richard McClure, on Right (2006)
The Massed Bands of The Coldstream and The Scots Guards
  Joined by the Army Band From Chile (2006)
The Three Tattoo Producers:
  Melville Jameson (Royal Edinburgh Military Tattoo),
  Erik Julliard (Basel Tattoo) and
  Brigadier Alfrey (Royal Edinburgh Military Tattoo) (2007)
Canadian Mounties at Windsor (2007)
Royal Arrival by Carriage, Windsor (2007)
Tank Commander Melville Jameson (2007)
HRH The Princess Royal, Tattoo Rehearsals, Redford Barracks (2007)
Massed Pipes and Drums Rehearsing Outside
  St Basil's Cathedral, Moscow, for the Kremlin Zoria Tattoo (2007)
Fireworks Over Red Square at the Finale of the
  Kremlin Ziora Tattoo (2007)

'Farewell to the Greys', The Pipes and Drums and Military Band
  of The Royal Scots Dragoon Guards (1972/1995) LP Record
7" Single of 'Amazing Grace'
The Edinburgh Military Tattoo Programme, 2001
The Edinburgh Military Tattoo Programme, 2003
The Edinburgh Military Tattoo Programme, 2006
Brigadier Sir Melville Jameson

ACKNOWLEDGEMENTS

We are exceedingly grateful to HRH The Princess Royal, The Royal Edinburgh Military Tattoo's Royal Patron, for her annual visits and her constant support over twenty years.

In addition, I offer my sincere thanks to the following people for their contributions to The Tattoo's success story during my time as producer/chief executive:

Justin Adams (ex-BBC)
BBC Scotland
Ian Balfour and Alistair Hutton (Chief Stewards)
Brenda Banks
Major Hugh Cameron, MBE
Champagne Pol Roger
John Del Nero
Susan Dodds
Dewar's Whisky
Major James Erskine, MBE
Paula Farrer
Billy Forsyth, MBE
Ian Gordon, MBE
Lieutenant Colonel Nick Grace, OBE, RM
Colonel Richard Hambleton, TD
Colonel Alasdair Hutton, OBE, TD
Susan Lawton
Major Brian Leishman, MBE
Mark Owen (Official Tattoo Photographer)
Lieutenant Colonel David Price, OBE
Captain Stuart Samson, MBE
Alan Smith
John Smith (BBC)
Major Gavin Stoddart, BEM, MBE
Steve Walsh, MBE
Clara Wheelan

I am deeply grateful to the three Services - the Royal Navy, the British Army and the Royal Air Force for their support in terms of Military Bands, Pipes and Drums and much more, as well as the many others who have contributed to the success of The Tattoo. And to the following people who inspired and produced the other great shows:

Major General Simon Brooks-Ward, CVO, OBE, TD, VR
(Royal Windsor Horse Show)
Erik Julliard (Basel Tattoo)
Colonel Ian Fraser, OMM, CD, ONS (Nova Scotia Tattoo)
Vitaly Mironov (Kremlin Tattoo)
Dr Dimitry Fedosov (Kremlin Tattoo)

The Royal Edinburgh Military Tattoo is in now in its 75th year and goes from strength to strength entertaining 230,000 people on the esplanade of Edinburgh Castle each year and an estimated audience of 100 million through BBC World.

The cast of around 800 is mostly made up of our excellent Pipes and Drums, Military Bands and Acts from home and since its inception, it has also been hugely supported by The Commonwealth and performers from around the world.

As a spectator, it is not entirely obvious how much work and planning goes on behind the scenes to make the show so special. This book tells the story of the extensive travels of one particular Tattoo Producer, his meetings with various leaders and heads of state. Together with some amusing moments, it demonstrates the skill of negotiation and diplomacy required to entice the very best performers to travel across the world to Edinburgh and give their services free of charge for four weeks in August. It also highlights some of the historic moments of The Tattoo including the visit by Her Majesty The Queen in 2002.

The Royal Edinburgh Military Tattoo, with its magnificent backdrop of Edinburgh Castle, maintains its reputation as the world's premier Tattoo. It is also an essential flagship for Scottish tourism as well as contributing annually around £1 million to Service Charities and the Arts. All of this, in no small part, thanks to the author of this book, Mel Jameson.

Her Royal Highness, The Princess Royal
Buckingham Palace

FOREWORD
Brigadier David Allfrey, MBE, FRGS

I HAVE KNOWN Brigadier Sir Melville Jameson for over 40 years, as a soldier, as a producer, a chief executive, Lord-Lieutenant, mentor and friend. A one-of-a-kind personality, he has supported in large measure our national institutions, charities, local communities and countless individuals. His charm and easy manner have allowed him an extraordinary access to royal families, ministers, heads of armed services – our own and internationally – corporate leaders and personalities large and small.

His story is remarkable and while he tells his tales with humility and a light touch, I would encourage you to reflect on what lies behind his adventures. For 'Mel' Jameson is above all a fabulous ambassador and an example for traditional values and standards and, for old world courtesies and diplomacy, those qualities that have helped the United Kingdom sustain its position as a major global 'soft power' player.

Mel's life has centred on his love and interest in people. His military career was characterised by this and played out in his commands of The Royal Scots Dragoon Guards and 51 Highland Brigade; he was directed by the then General Officer Commanding Scotland, at short notice, to stand in as producer of the world-renowned Royal Edinburgh Military Tattoo. After delivering a successful show, he retired from the Army and took up the permanent position as chief executive and producer. He led the organisation for a successful and happy twelve years, building on the event's heritage while innovating and setting standards of professionalism and creativity that set The Tattoo as a world leader in live performance and television broadcast.

The Royal Edinburgh Military Tattoo is a 'hybrid' in that, while founded on volunteering and charity – supporting each year the Armed Forces and the Arts – it is also a crisp and innovative business that must make its way through ticket sales and sound commercial practice.

The show has been based traditionally on the expertise and showmanship of the United Kingdom's Armed Forces, reinforced with guest performances by international armed forces and folkloric groups.

It has tried to place a particular emphasis on friendships across The Commonwealth but is far from restricted to this. Indeed, The Tattoo – in common with many arts and cultural organisations – has sought to sustain relationships with countries even when political situations have been tense; Russia and China are cases in point.

The task of the producer/chief executive has been to recruit all these acts, differently each year, at the lowest possible cost but to the greatest impact and bring them together in a motivated, unified, and exhilarating show on the esplanade of Edinburgh Castle: a live audience of 8,800 each evening in August (220,000 annually) and a huge BBC audience at home and abroad. This, as well as acting as a cornerstone for the Scottish and British visitor economy, delivers around £120 million in 'additionality' each year.

To do this efficiently and effectively, the producer/chief executive must draw deeply on their creative spirit, a professional understanding of the resources needed to deliver a mega-event and the skills and emotional quotient of leadership and management – these tuned to the culture and manners of each country involved.

When successful, this blend creates a rich collaboration connecting sailors, soldiers, aviators, folk groups, traditional dancers and musicians, technical expertise, event management and business support staff – some paid, some volunteers. At its best, it is not only a fabulous experience for the audience and the City of Edinburgh but is also unforgettable for all those taking part.

Joseph Nye defined 'soft power' as 'the ability to affect others to obtain the outcomes one wants through attraction rather than coercion or payment. A country's soft power rests on its resources of culture, values, and policies'. Accordingly, The Royal Edinburgh Military Tattoo offers a unique opportunity to 'shape' the boundaries between hard and soft power in setting up military and other international performers to represent – and be representatives of – their nations. It is a fabulous shop window and Mel Jameson used his skills and experiences as a soldier, showman and diplomat to make the very best of this opportunity for over a decade.

As you read Mel Jameson's life adventure, enjoy the story for all its joy, variety and colour and, at the same time, reflect on how he has contributed with creativity.

PREFACE

A MILITARY TATTOO is a performance of military music or a display of armed forces normally held in the evening or at night. The term comes from the early seventeenth-century Dutch phrase *doe den tap toe* ('turn off the tap'), a signal sounded by drummers or trumpeters to instruct innkeepers near military garrisons to stop serving beer and for soldiers to return to their barracks.

Over the years the process became a more formal show of Military Bands and displays often conducted by floodlight or searchlight. Tattoos were commonplace in the late nineteenth century, with most military and garrison towns in England putting on some kind of show or entertainment during the summer months. Between the First World War and the Second World War, more elaborate military tattoos were held in many garrison towns and cities, with the largest held in Aldershot.

The Royal Edinburgh Military Tattoo was conceived in 1949 as the Army in Scotland's contribution to The Edinburgh International Festival and was first performed in 1950; it was agreed that a financial contribution would be made to the Edinburgh Festival and any surplus would be donated to Service Charities; that practice has been continued to this day – so The Royal Edinburgh Military Tattoo is now 75 years old.

The Tattoo, unlike the other festivals, survives on ticket income and not government subsidy and has always covered its costs despite looking after a cast of around 800 every year over three weeks. In recent years, it has annually donated around £1 million to Service Charities and the Arts.

The Tattoo has been sold out since 2000 and the demand for tickets has been huge. The show goes from strength to strength with an exciting cast of bands and acts from home, The Commonwealth and all over the world. Times are ever changing, but the public demand for Pipe Bands, Military Bands, Highland Dancing as well as pomp and circumstance, set against the finest backdrop of Edinburgh Castle, remains undiminished.

Mel Jameson, April 2025

INTRODUCTION

TOWARDS THE END of my military career with my regiment, The Royal Scots Dragoon Guards, I was honoured to be invited to command the 51st Highland Brigade – the successor to the famous 51st Highland Division which earned itself such a formidable reputation throughout two world wars. It was made up of the revered and most distinguished Highland Regiments of Scotland and other units.

In 1993, the 51st Highland Brigade headquarters was comfortably situated in two beautiful Georgian houses on the South Inch of the city of Perth. The Command consisted of the Highlands and Islands of Scotland and all the military formations and assets therein. I was the first cavalry officer appointed to command this infantry brigade so it was a privilege indeed. Furthermore, I was able to live at my family home near Blairgowrie where I was born, despite the offer of the rather palatial brigadier's residence on Kinnoull Hill in Perth. My family, Sarah and our two sons, Harry and Michael, were delighted to be home at last after all those years of postings worldwide and some fifteen different houses and Army quarters.

I was generously allocated a Staff Car and a fine driver, Corporal Ian Campbell, a piper from The Royal Scots Dragoon Guards, and, at home, a House Sergeant, Len Kerr, who had served with me since the 1960s and was extremely skilled after years serving in the Officers' Mess. As my territory measured some 450 miles in length – Shetland to Galloway – and 150 miles across as well as the Western Isles, I was also able to call upon a Gazelle helicopter when necessary from the 3 Flight Army Air Corps commanded by the very accomplished pilot, Major Andrew Gordon, which was based at RAF Leuchars. The Gazelle would land on the lawn in front of my house and then take me on various official flights offering en route stunning views such as the Cairngorms and the Lairig Ghru mountain pass to Inverness. Importantly, it allowed me to make frequent visits to regular, reserve and cadet units in all parts of the Highlands and Islands.

Accordingly, I was well ensconced by the end of my first year and looking forward to continuing this extremely busy but really enjoyable lifestyle – very much 'my own boss' or so I thought. Then, on a Friday afternoon in December 1994, everything changed. My excellent PA, Anne Amos, burst into my office to tell me that the GOC (Major General Mike Scott, General Officer Commanding Scotland) wanted to see me immediately.

'I can't believe it,' I said to Anne. 'On a Friday afternoon, most unusual, it must be very urgent; maybe war has been declared.'

I set off at speed with my driver, Corporal Campbell, to HQ Scotland then based at Craigiehall just north of Edinburgh.

On arrival in the General's outer office, the aide-de-camp said the General wants to see you straight away and quickly ushered me through to his office without the customary cup of coffee which did not bode well.

'Sit down, Mel, sit down.'

At that point, I was on the edge of my seat.

'You may not be aware that The Tattoo producer has resigned due to ill health.' The General continued, 'I would like you to produce The Edinburgh Military Tattoo next year.'

Somewhat shocked, I said, 'I beg your pardon, General.'

'Yes Mel, The Edinburgh Tattoo.'

'What about my brigade?' I asked.

He smiled and replied, 'Mel, I am sure you will manage!'

Knowing The Tattoo was just seven months away this looked like somewhat of a challenge, but I judged this to be 'a command' so I rose to my feet, saluted smartly and said, 'Thank you so much General.'

The reason for my instant appointment was that the previous producer, Major Sir Michael Parker, had sadly resigned for health reasons. Michael was renowned as the distinguished producer of The Royal Tournament in London as well as many high-profile Royal events including The Queen's Golden Jubilee, so assuming the mantle from him was a daunting prospect.

Thus began a new phase in my life, balancing the many Brigade commitments and gearing up for The Tattoo in August to an expected audience of 220,000, a BBC following of around four million in the UK and a huge international audience through BBC World. Later, I was informed that in Australia and New Zealand, the Christmas Day routine for families was to watch The Queen's Speech then The Royal Edinburgh Military Tattoo, which was for many a much-loved glimpse of home.

CHAPTER 1
1995

LIKE MOST PEOPLE living in Scotland, I knew The Edinburgh Tattoo extremely well both as a child and as a soldier. My regiment had supported the show since the very beginning providing its excellent Military Band and Pipes and Drums and sometimes armoured cars or a mounted troop of grey horses. I was lucky to be appointed Pipe President and later Band President so I had also attended the show in an official capacity many times and, by chance, I was closely associated with our 'Amazing Grace' recording success in 1972.

'Amazing Grace' became a 'battle honour' for the regiment and an extraordinary event in our history. Prior to the amalgamation of the regiment in 1971, we recorded an LP with RCA Records, called 'Farewell to the Greys', which consisted of all the regimental music of The Royal Scots Dragoon Guards. At the end of the recording session in Edinburgh, there was still some room on the LP so it was reluctantly agreed by RCA that we would include this newly-arranged track, 'Amazing Grace', which was the inspiration of the then Pipe Sergeant Tony Crease (later Pipe Major and Major Crease) and arranged by our Bandmaster, Stuart Fairbairn; and, with one take only, it was 'in the can'. Then, in the spring of 1972, it was picked up by Ian Fenner, the producer of the BBC's 'Late Night Extra' programme. 'Amazing Grace' was played just once on BBC2 and went straight into the pop charts staying at number 1 for five weeks resulting in us all performing at the Top of The Pops Studio in London. The Pipes and Drums and Military Band were by then superstars earning eight gold discs and greatly in demand by the media, performing at 'The Royal Variety Performance' and followed by extensive worldwide band tours. However, despite this exciting introduction to show business, I had no experience of organising a tattoo or a show of such size and importance.

This being December, I assumed that the bands and acts would be already booked, so I telephoned the business manager, Major Brian Leishman, who I knew, to identify the plans and programme for 1995. Brian had served with the Cameronians and King's Own Scottish Borderers.

'I'm sorry to tell you that the larder is empty,' he said. 'However, we have the promise of a couple of Pipes and Drums and maybe the Welsh Guards Band but not much else,' he went on to say. 'Oh, but there is a theme already advertised, "The House of Stewart" – there is a lot of work to be done,' he added.

That was not quite the encouraging news I was hoping for so, after Christmas, I urgently set about putting a show together.

Because of the theme that I inherited, I became an instant expert on 'The House of Stewart, Joan of Arc and Bonnie Prince Charlie', but how was I to portray this on the Esplanade of Edinburgh Castle? Firstly, however, I needed to put together an interesting cast. I had been informed that Egypt might be interested in participating, not a lot to do with the House of Stewart, but without any other options on the table, I flew to Cairo where the Defence Attaché had organised a programme and what a programme! I was comfortably accommodated in the *Sheraton Hotel* although I did not see much of it. Luckily, I was still a serving officer so I was in full uniform and, as a British officer, I was treated like royalty.

The Egyptian Army could not have been more hospitable and friendly. On the first day, I met the Chief of the Army and then many senior generals, all fascinated about The Tattoo and at every meeting, was offered delicious tea, coffee and a large quantity of cake as is the custom – by the evening my uniform was busting at the seams.

Finally, I saw a performance by the Egyptian Army Band and Pipes and Drums (still going since the British left Egypt) on a vast parade ground. Most interesting was the gait of the Pipes and Drums: a swaying from side to side – I was gripped by this but not their playing or the uniform. At night, I was invited to see a stage show with them all dressed impressively in Pharaonic costume – I was then persuaded that they would fit the bill and I invited them, as long as they all dressed as Pharaohs. They did exactly that and in August, 80 bandsmen dressed as Pharaohs arrived in Edinburgh, accompanied by Pharaoh Ramses 11 in a golden chariot, which became central to their act.

While I was in Cairo, I was determined to see the Pyramids but the traffic was bedlam during the day, however, woken by 'the call to prayer' from the mosque outside my bedroom, I made a dawn visit to Giza. The Pyramids in the morning sunlight were stunning and deserted except for a few camels and then on my way back to the city, I had a brief meeting with the Pharaoh Tutankhamen at the Cairo Museum.

On my return to Edinburgh, I was delighted to hear that the French had also agreed to join us with La Musique du 42nd Regiment de Transmission. So with a good selection of Pipe Bands and Military Bands, we had a show coming together.

In May, I was contacted by an old friend from Nova Scotia who had served with The Canadian Black Watch, Colonel Ian Fraser and who I had met when serving with the United Nations in Cyprus in the 1970s. He was the producer of The Nova Scotia Tattoo in Halifax.

His fax message read, *'I see you have been appointed as Producer for The Edinburgh Military Tattoo – you may need my help'*.

This was an understatement! I completely agreed so I accepted his kind invitation to visit his show in July despite the fact the date was rather close to my rehearsals. I spent some days in Halifax with Ian and his team who were so kind and helpful and Ian showed me 'the ropes'. The Nova Scotia Tattoo was started by Ian Fraser having learnt his skills from the revered Brigadier Alistair Maclean one of the early producers of The Edinburgh Tattoo. I was so impressed by this show; it was the shop window for the Canadian Military and Scottish Culture, and run with military precision. It was fast-moving, fun and had wonderful music. I learnt so much from this, Nova Scotia became our sister show and I visited every year during my tenure at Edinburgh.

Perhaps the most alarming moment for the producer is the rehearsals and the run-up to the show. You have just four days until the very public dress rehearsal and press preview. We rehearse from 7 am to midnight, which is exhausting, and my first Monday was chaotic: interpreting the theme was challenging, the well-known Tattoo advice is *'Never have horses and children'* and we had both! The climax on Monday night was the appearance of Joan of Arc in full armour (played by Lieutenant Plum Anderson from the Scottish Yeomanry) mounted on her large grey charger.

As she crossed the drawbridge of Edinburgh Castle looking magnificent, the charger who was naturally nervous, alarmingly reared up in fright and galloped down the esplanade and the Royal Mile never to be seen again that night! So when we got to the rehearsal post-mortem of the day at midnight in the Castle, there was a distinct aura of gloom and doom from the more experienced Tattoo staff members.

There were comments like, 'We told you horses would not work on The Tattoo'. And I could see them thinking, 'Who on earth selected this person as producer'.

I thought to myself this is the classic 'poisoned chalice'. Then at the end of a most depressing session, I asked my BBC producer, Justin Adams, who I had just met, what he thought of the day's rehearsals. He kindly said, 'Mel you have a great show coming together here!' This was both charming and encouraging and it was greatly appreciated. Justin became a good friend and a key part of The Tattoo Production Team.

Day two, Tuesday was a revelation and to see the finesse and majesty of the Welsh Guards and the Massed Pipes and Drums cross the drawbridge just filled one with confidence!

Everything seemed to work well which was largely due to my Production Manager, Steve Walsh (ex-Gordon Highlanders and ex-Castle RSM). I was very lucky to have Steve, he had a great eye for detail and an extraordinary gift of getting the very best out of all the acts. Furthermore, he was greatly respected and popular with the cast.

The dress rehearsal with a local and very critical Scottish audience (half-price tickets) as well as the press and media, went surprisingly well and the relief was indescribable. Nonetheless, there were some interesting remarks.

A senior officer said to me, 'That tune Sancerre went on rather a long time,' to which I replied, 'That tune was from Saint-Saens I think you will find that Sancerre is a bottle of wine.'

A well-known consul general's wife who was more a follower of the Edinburgh International Festival, when I asked what she had liked best, after thinking hard said, 'I much enjoyed the firework music.' This was a classical piece from a CD.

Sarah my wife became my 'arch critic'. She would attend the Wednesday rehearsal in the arena after which I would hear her detailed views on the show, hopefully complimentary, but always, over the years, really useful to me.

The other idea she had was to have a 'heads of cast' lunch on a free day over the weekend. We started with around twelve in the dining room at home and the number gradually increased every year until we were feeding

60 with a BBQ in the walled garden with a hog roast. Our guests were all great characters from The Commonwealth and around the world. It was our opportunity to thank them and get to know them better.

My friend and Helicopter Flight Commander, Major Andrew Gordon, heard of our lunches and offered a Gazelle helicopter to take some of our guests to my home 60 miles north of Edinburgh – the rest would travel in a bus. As the years progressed, we had four Gazelles deployed to assist and they would land on our lawn – the pilots joining the lunch. They would then take some of the guests back to Redford Barracks, Edinburgh. Apparently, when the General Officer Commanding Scotland used to ask for a helicopter on this particular day, he would be informed that all the helicopters were unavailable as they were on a special training mission – little did he know!

The most important development of that year, however, was the formation of a small but outstanding in-house team who were all passionate about The Tattoo and they so greatly contributed to the success of the future decade and were also great fun to work with.

CHAPTER 2
1996

FOR THE NEXT TATTOO, I inherited another theme from my predecessor and that was the 'The Bicentenary Celebration of Robert Burns'. Consequently, this show would feature vignettes of his extraordinary life but for me and The Tattoo what was so very appropriate and enjoyable for this occasion was the music that surrounded Scotland's literary legend. These included:

'The Star of Robert Burns'
'Bonnie Wee Thing'
'A Man's a Man for a' That'
And many more.

With the experience of one show, I had worked out a basic blueprint for The Tattoo to concentrate the mind – in the Army, I was taught the wisdom of a simple plan. The four main pillars of The Tattoo:

The Massed Pipes and Drums Emerging from the drawbridge, never in future to be less than ten bands.
The Massed Military Bands Drawn from the Army, Navy and Air Force.
Variety in the Middle With Highland Dancing and other bands, cultural groups and acts from home and overseas.
The Finale A massive spectacle of light and sound – a musical climax of Military Bands and Pipes and Drums playing combined music against the stunning backdrop of the Castle ramparts.

A very experienced Tattoo follower I met at that time showing little enthusiasm for my first show said to me, 'Of course it doesn't really matter what you do on the esplanade – people really come to see the "Son et Lumiere" on the Castle.'
'How kind and reassuring,' I thought!

The Massed Pipes and Drums had been the mainstay and focus of The Tattoo for over 50 years alongside the lone piper. I was determined to have an apposite-sized Massed Pipes and Drums as up to this point, it had been between four and seven bands – really quite small.

This was a real challenge: in a steadily decreasing British Army, how could this be achieved? I was aware that, as with much of Scottish culture, there were Pipes and Drums spread around the world most particularly in The Commonwealth. The best quality Pipes and Drums are to be found mainly in Canada, Australia, New Zealand and South Africa; some of these bands had been to The Tattoo before but now we were going to invite many more to join us.

I was most fortunate to have the talented Major Gavin Stoddart, BEM, MBE, Director Army Bagpipe Music, who would create the musical programme and assemble a Massed Pipes and Drums, the biggest ever at The Tattoo with bands from Canada and Hong Kong. Gavin's father, Pipe Major Stoddart, had before him been the lone piper for the first eleven years of The Tattoo. Thanks to Gavin, I never had to worry about the quality of the Massed Pipes and Drums performance.

I was also delighted to hear that the excellent Scots Guards Military Band had been appointed as the lead Military Band for 1996 with their Director of Music, Lieutenant Colonel David Price, OBE, Senior Director of Music for the Army, one of the few directors of music who understood the Highland bagpipes and was a talented arranger of combined music (Military Bands with Pipes and Drums).

I had also discussed Highland Dancing with the well-known Tattoo Dance Director, Billy Forsyth.

'Why such a modest amount (twenty) of dancers in past Tattoos?' I queried.

We agreed to go for 50 and create a more formal choreographed Highland Dancing act. The concept of Massed Highland dancing, I am pleased to say, really caught on as I will describe in a later chapter with the climax of 200 Highland dancers in Australia and New Zealand in 2000 and 2005.

So it was time to find some overseas acts to add some spice to the show. I was aware there were some excellent Military Bands in the US Army, and so, with the help of the British Defence and Liaison Staff and some

CHAPTER 2 - 1996

contacts, I flew to Washington DC. They say that if you mean business, stay in the smartest hotel. With that in mind, I was booked into *The Willard* (200 years old and known as the 'Residence of Presidents') which is situated a stone's throw from the White House. I visited The Old Guard (3rd US Infantry Regiment, a contingent consisting of three battalions). The Old Guard is the US Army's official ceremonial unit and 'The Escort to The President'.

I was given a full tour of this extraordinary regiment which has the responsibility for all US Army ceremonies in the capital and at Arlington Cemetery for military funerals. The main ceremonial elements include:

United States Army Band (Pershing's Own) A world-class band with about 250 musicians including orchestras, choirs and much more.
United States Army Drill Team An extraordinary silent drill display team.
United States Army Caisson Platoon A unit which provides the horses and caissons for carrying the caskets for military funerals.
Continental Color Guard Used for ceremonial functions.
United States Army Old Guard Fife and Drum Corps Dressed in the traditional uniforms of the American Revolution of 1784, the Corps is highly drilled and performs cutting-edge fife and drums music.
Specialist platoons used for guarding the 'Unknown Soldier'.

It was all extremely impressive. In the end, I invited Pershing's Own Band (some 80 of them) and the Drill Team and received an early agreement from the two-star general and Commander; this was the special relationship at work I thought. I gave lunch at the *Old Ebbitt Grill* for them – the Director of Music and the leader of the Drill Team – and flew home delighted, saying to myself that was easy.

By May, however, I was getting concerned as I had not had the final formal agreement which was sitting with the Pentagon. By chance, I had been invited to the US Army's Military show – an indoor Tattoo entitled 'The Spirit of America' and so flew back to Washington for one night to see their show knowing that I had to get an answer. No one met me at the airport so I took a taxi to *The Willard* knowing that I had little time to change for the evening show. As I reached my hotel room, the Colonel, my contact with the Old Guard, rang to say he was picking me up in twenty minutes, so I leapt into full Number 1 Dress/Blues and went off to the show. En route, I enquired with the Colonel about my invitation to The Tattoo, he said there was as yet no confirmation. He warned me that the show would be full of top brass, senior generals from the Pentagon, and I was not to mention The Tattoo as they have not yet been briefed. This was somewhat disappointing news.

The first half of the show depicted the War of Independence, which did not fill me with great joy and I pretended to be asleep. So then spurred on and undaunted, during the interval I approached the first four-star US general. He asked who I was in this strange cavalry uniform, so I explained that I came from Scotland's senior regiment and I produced a show called The Royal Edinburgh Military Tattoo. Then I said how very grateful I was that the Old Guard would be coming to Edinburgh in August for The Edinburgh Military Tattoo, Great Britain's largest military musical event and seen by millions around the world.

He paused and said, 'I have not been briefed on this one. You better come to my office tomorrow.'

And so that was that and I enjoyed the second part of the show!

Next morning, with some trepidation, I set off for the Pentagon, the headquarters of the US Defence Department, the largest office in the world covering 29 acres and with 17 miles of corridor and somewhat challenging to navigate. On arrival, I was made aware that my meeting was with the very senior and important Vice-Chief of the Defence Staff, General Griffith. I could not get much higher!

At the end of my interview, he put his hand on my shoulder and said to me, 'General, I am committed to your invitation – leave it with me.'

Mission accomplished, but it was too close for comfort as they represented a huge part of the programme.

My next adventure was South Africa. We have all seen the great film *Zulu* and I was keen to bring Zulus to Edinburgh. This was my first visit to South Africa and on my way I read *Shaka Zulu King of the Zulus*, who created the formidable Zulu empire through his ferocious and well-trained army. Fortunately, my admiration for the Zulu was rewarded with meeting them in Durban with the South African Police who had agreed to form a Zulu display team. We rehearsed the act and, as the only non-South African present, surrounded by these mighty warriors, it became somewhat unnerving! Later, The South African Police flew me over Durban and pointed out the shanty towns where Zulus had migrated from their nice villages to find a new life but ended in a slum.

The press and media in Edinburgh, to my annoyance, had under my watch largely ignored The Tattoo on the esplanade of the previous year – they seemed to consider The Tattoo old hat, military and boring yet gave wonderful accolades to the more fashionable International Festival and Edinburgh Fringe. I was determined to change this.

Accordingly, while they were en route to Edinburgh, I told the Zulus to change clothes – into loin cloth and spear – and informed the press and media of their arrival. The next day we had the front page of all the newspapers and even BBC coverage: 'Edinburgh was being invaded by the Zulus'.

The 1996 show was a huge improvement on the previous year, the highlights being:

The very cool silent drill from the *US Army Drill Team* tossing rifles.

Stirring music from the outstanding *Pershing's Own Band* including at my request Glen Miller's 'In the Mood' and 'America the Beautiful'.

A great joint band finale and the best rendition of 'Highland Cathedral' ever heard. This was a *Scots Guards* arrangement conducted with great skill by our Senior Director of Music, Lieutenant Colonel David Price, OBE, who became a great friend and my musical adviser and arranger.

The finale was also brilliantly painted by the celebrated artist Hugo Grenville which he titled appropriately 'Highland Cathedral'.

CHAPTER 3
1997

I HAD NOW decided against the employment of artistic themes, which are difficult to execute well on the large esplanade (which measured 90 m by 25 m) and was advised that some 30 per cent of our international guests could not easily understand the theme storyline. In future, I would concentrate on major themes such as royal anniversaries, HM The Queen's Golden Jubilee (2002) and, in 1997, it would be the Golden Wedding Anniversary of HM The Queen and Prince Philip. The key players were booked embracing three bands from Her Majesty's Royal Marines, ten Pipes and Drums including two excellent bands from Australia – the West Australia Police Pipe Band and The Rats of Tobruk Memorial Pipes and Drums.

A new problem was developing for Tattoos – the celebrated acts from the three Services that used to perform at The Royal Tournament and Tattoos such as The Royal Navy Gun Run, the RAF Police Dogs, Royal Navy display teams and military gymnastic display teams, were now, due to defence cuts, difficult to find or did not exist anymore. That said, for some, they were a bit 'old hat'.

Following the horrors of the Second World War, The Edinburgh Tattoo was designed to show off to the public the 'scarlet, gold, musical and ceremonial' image of the British Armed Forces. My plan for the future, therefore, was to find the most interesting and exciting acts and bands from home and from overseas.

Sadly, my excellent personal assistant, Pixie Campbell, MBE, who I had inherited from Michael Parker, decided to retire. I was lucky, however, to be offered Brenda Banks who had been PA to Brian Leishman for many years. She worked miracles looking after my life and was central in organising my extensive and complicated travels which continued for ten years, starting with my first long and substantial overseas tour around the world for four weeks.

In Trinidad and Tobago, I spoke to the Defence Adviser for The West Indies about my need to find a Military Steel Band. *Was there one?*

The Defence Advisor informed me that, by chance, the Defence Force of Trinidad and Tobago had just converted their Military Band into a Steel Band. I asked for a visit and this was not a bad way to start my tour, as Trinidad and Tobago in March is a very nice place to be! I had a wonderful visit to Trinidad which is the main island, next door is Tobago, the stunning holiday island. Of course, Steel Bands originated from Trinidad and the capital, Port of Spain, in around 1940 for the Carnival and then was emulated by many West Indian islands.

I was taken to meet the High Commissioner and then the Chief of Defence Staff, Brigadier Carl Alfonso, who took me to see his new Steel Band. I arrived on the parade ground as the band appeared in smart white uniforms. They were playing tunes such as 'British Grenadiers' and 'Stars and Stripes from Sousa' and as with an infantry Military Band they had a row of drums in front.

None of this was what I expected so I rather boldly asked, 'Please could we have some Caribbean music and perhaps remove the very loud infantry drums?'

Having suggested some tunes that would go down well at home, I visited rehearsals and watched those talented musicians learning tunes by ear and, in just one session, we had a very special Steel Band, playing the tunes we all love so much, such as 'Island in the Sun', 'Brown Girl in the Ring' and 'Yellow Bird High up in Banana Tree'. They were a huge success in Edinburgh and the audience loved them. The Tattoo in Edinburgh was for them a springboard for invitations later to Tattoos all over the world and even Windsor where they performed before The Queen.

The next stop was Barbados, the most beautiful Caribbean island. Heavily defended by forts and cannons in the days of the British Empire because of the sugar cane trade, Barbados is an island with the most stunning white beaches. It was never conquered by the French and remained loyal to the monarchy during the time of Oliver Cromwell.

The British Defence Adviser of The West Indies must have the best job in the world. He took me to see the Commander of the Defence Force, Brigadier Lewis. His band is known as the Zouave Band due to its wonderful uniform comprising a red Fez, white Turban and a scarlet sleeveless jacket, which originated from the French Army tradition and became the uniform of The West Indian Regiment.

I attended a rehearsal – the uniform was brilliant, but the musical quality was not so good. I asked the Brigadier if we could add steel pans. He was horrified and gruffly said that Barbados had never used such common instruments! I got the message.

Nonetheless, I booked them for 1999 anyway; I diarised to check them on my visit the following year.

I continued my journey via Los Angeles which was quite a contrast with the charm of Barbados. I was en route to Fiji.

This very special group of islands is Melanesian as opposed to Polynesian. The men are huge and perfect for rugby, the women beautiful with frizzy hair and quite different from their Polynesian cousins. From my arrival at Nadi (pronounced Nandi), I received the warmest welcome. My hotel, *The Sheraton*, was very comfortable, my bedroom literally on the beach, white sand and warm turquoise sea.

Fiji has had a very close relationship with Britain over many years with Fijians serving as soldiers in the Second World War (The Fiji Regiment) and more recently in the British Army and also in the SAS.

I flew down to Suva, the capital, to join my good friend, Colonel Peter Barry, the Defence Adviser, who had kindly organised my visit. We went firstly to the High Commissioner, then to the Queen Elizabeth Barracks to meet the Commander Fiji Forces and also to see the Forces' Band in rehearsal at the barracks. The Director of Music was Captain Luki Temani who had performed at The Edinburgh Tattoo years before as a musician – a talented and charming man.

The visit started with the 'Kava Ceremony' – a new experience for me and the traditional greeting in Fiji. Kava is made from the Yaqona root and is mildly narcotic, relaxing and leaves a numb feeling around the mouth. However, at first sight, it looks like brown dishwater.

After sitting down with the whole contingent, the Director of Music offered me the Kava in a full coconut cup.

'You clap once and shout *Bulla* (Hello). Drink the whole cup and clap three times and shout *Maca!*'

Still alive after that, I witnessed these wonderful and fierce warriors dancing a *meke* wearing grass skirts. The band, however, were dressed in the renowned Fiji full dress uniform of a red tunic and white Sulu (skirt) – without a hat – and sandals. I was so taken by their music and their talented singing in harmony, particularly their island song 'Isa-lei', which was haunting and beautiful.

I next met the Commander, General Ganilau MC, who was trained at The Royal Military Academy Sandhurst. We got on famously and over lunch in the very civilised Officers' Mess, I requested the band for 1998. He was keen and in support of the proposal. He even arranged for me to meet the Fijian Prime Minister, Sitiveni Rabuka.

Before I left Suva, I was walking near to my hotel and came across a very small and quaint church. Its sign described it simply as 'The Church of Scotland'. It is tiny but charming, with a wicker gate and a palm tree on each side – memorable. They have many churches in Fiji and they are all full on Sunday.

With some good luck, I left Fiji just hours before a massive cyclone hit the island creating much damage.

Next, it was my first visit to New Zealand. A home from home and in so many ways like Scotland. Colonel Peter Barry, the Defence Attaché, had once again planned an extensive and fascinating programme for me. My main aim here was to establish a strong link with their Pipes and Drums Association and to meet their Highland dancers who I had heard were excellent.

I flew into Dunedin (*Dùn Èideann* – the Gaelic for Edinburgh) and had no problem finding my way as the streets, Princes Street, George Street and Queen Street, were laid out just the same as Edinburgh.

The first item on my programme was to meet Pipes and Drums at the New Zealand Championships at Invercargill, situated at the bottom of the South Island. I was accommodated at Bluff Cove, originally called Campbelltown, at the very extremity of the South Island after which there is only sea for 3,000 miles down to the South Pole. It is not unlike John O'Groats with rough seas and plentiful seaweed and, like a normal Scottish day in mid-summer, it was raining as we arrived at the Invercargill Pipe Band Championships. As with Highland gatherings in Scotland, there were white tents, judges, the sound of pipes everywhere and, of course, Highland dancing. I felt completely at home.

I then was introduced to the President, Nigel Foster, who looked unimpressed by my non-Highland dress.

'Who are you?' he asked.

I rather reservedly responded, 'I produce a show called The Royal Edinburgh Military Tattoo. It takes place every year in August.'

The President was speechless.

I was, thereafter, treated like royalty and received a wonderfully warm welcome over two days: lunches, drams and just typical Kiwi friendship.

The whole performance was hugely impressive with great bands, superb playing and, on the Sunday – with it still raining to create the right atmosphere – I was invited to present the silver medals in the presence of 50 Pipes and Drums, and make a speech. It was all a great honour and this heralded a very close and important relationship for The Tattoo with New Zealand thereafter. I invited two excellent Grade 1 bands for The 1998 Tattoo, Invercargill and Dunedin, both from cities celebrating 150 years and who gave us a professional display of piping.

I noticed at the championships a familiar uniform.

'Could it be The Black Watch all the way Down Under?', I wondered.

I tapped the Pipe Major on the shoulder.

'Good Morning, Pipey.'

Pipe Major WO1 Stevie Small, Black Watch, who I knew well from The Tattoo, turned around not expecting to see anyone checking them out from home.

In shock, he said, 'Oh no!'

He later went on to perform very well in Grade 1. Major Steven Small, MBE, is today Performance Director for The Tattoo.

The next city in the programme was Wellington and, as I found out, certainly earned its nickname of 'Windy Wellington'. As I was leaving my hotel for a meeting – outside it was raining and I noticed there was a high wind – I seized a hotel umbrella and, as I was at the front door struggling to put my umbrella up to brave the weather, a local walking past me smiled and said, 'And the best of luck to you, Mate.' He was right. The umbrella turned inside out at once.

I had my first meeting with the Chief of Army regarding the New Zealand Army Band which first came to the show in 2000. Their claim to fame was talented 'musical comedy on the march' and the Haka, of course. They later became Tattoo superstars, forever greatly in demand.

I also had the pleasure of meeting Colleen Pobar, the well-known director of the all-women Lochiel Drill Team, which had been to

Edinburgh before, and I invited them again.

My final joy was when I discovered Shed 5 in the old port where I gave lunch to the Defence Attaché and others. Shed 5 and the Dockside are two excellent restaurants in the old port where, over the years, I had many lunch meetings and where good business was carried out over fine New Zealand wine and the largest fish and chips in the world.

On departing, the Defence Attaché asked me, 'Have you been to the Cook Islands?'

I said I had not considered it as there was no military there.

'Ah,' he said, 'but there are wonderful Polynesian dancers.'

I made a mental note and began my journey to Australia.

This was my first visit to Australia and it was to Adelaide City. On visiting the Lord Mayor in the city chambers, he informed me that this beautiful city by the River Torrens had been designed by Colonel William Light, Royal Engineers, in around 1836 using a grid system. Colonel Light designed the main streets to be wide, which he said would make cannonball fire less effective.

I was honoured to meet Sir Eric Neil, the Governor of South Australia, in the very grand Governor's Mansion and, as I was driven down the drive, I noticed the Governor's personal mounted escort from the South Australia Police on fine grey horses. After the presentations and formal chat, he invited me to lunch. On the way into the Grand Dining Room, I passed wall-to-wall full-length portraits of the Royal Family from yesteryear.

I was expecting a rather formal stuffy lunch but, in true Australian style, he said, 'We are having my favourite dish today – Australian Whiting and Chips.'

It was excellent.

Later, I met and witnessed a display by the South Australia Police Band – all brass and a neatly choreographed act with plenty of humour. I asked them to attend Edinburgh in 2000. In addition, I was able to meet informally the Mounted Police Troop of Grey Horses. I also met the Adelaide University Pipe and Drums who had already attended The Tattoo.

In the afternoon, I was taken to the Adelaide Wine Festival and given a tour of various familiar vineyards such as Jacob's Creek and Penfolds. We tasted great wine. Australia keeps all the best for itself.

CHAPTER 3 - 1997

My final destination was another first for me. I was visiting as an official guest of the Pakistan Army to find a Pipes and Drums or a Military Band and possibly a cultural act. It was a very long flight indeed, the total flight via Singapore, Karachi and Islamabad was 22 hours. The last leg by Pakistan Airways was not quite the standard of British Airways and very casual: there were people smoking on take-off and spread across the seats without seat belts. Then we experienced ferocious turbulence and this was one of those occasions that I was extremely grateful to land. On arrival, I was somewhat surprised that there was no reception committee as I was a guest of the Pakistan Army. I think they got the flights wrong. Hence, I set off in a delightful and very old Morris Minor taxi – so small that my large suitcase was stuck out of the boot. My hotel was *The Pearl Continental* at Rawalpindi, 'the Aldershot' of Pakistan, which I soon identified to my horror was dry as is Pakistan – so the next seven days were very good for my health.

I was settling down in my room with a Coca-Cola after such a long and unpleasant flight, exhausted, when there was a knock on the door. This was my guide, the charming Major Shabbir. He was appalled that he had missed me at the airport and offered his services.

'Sahib, anything you would like to do. The car is outside at your disposal.'

I had just received a fax from my wife, Sarah, who asked if I could find some Kilim rugs/carpets when in Pakistan. So, no time like the present and in order not to disappoint my guide, I asked Shabbir if we could go to a carpet shop. As I departed the hotel lobby, outside to my complete surprise was a massive convoy including a motorcycle escort, a Military Police Land Rover and a very large black Staff Car all with sirens sounding and red lights flashing. I began to think my shopping spree was probably not quite what was expected of this foreign visitor; the carpet shop was only just around the corner and we travelled with sirens blaring. It turned out to be domestic carpets – so the trip was aborted but we did a bit of sightseeing in the dark.

My visit to Pakistan was memorable and I was shown remarkable hospitality and kindness everywhere I went. I will endeavour to cover some of the highlights.

As stated earlier, my aim was to find a Military Band or a Pipes and

Drums and some cultural acts such as dancing. I was summoned to a meeting with the Pakistan Army Deputy Director Personal Services and the British Defence Adviser, Brigadier Digby O'Lone. They suggested that I should see the Pipes and Drums of the 8th Independent Kashmir Regiment – Number 1 in Pakistan – and then they would arrange a trip up the Khyber Pass for me to see the Khyber dancers from the old British-named regiment, The Khyber Rifles.

That evening, I was invited to dinner with the Defence Adviser and was offered a large whisky – the best I had ever tasted after my very dry start.

The next day, I visited the Pipes and Drums of the 8th Kashmir Independent Regiment, the winners of the Pakistan Pipe Band Championships. They played well, had a superb uniform and an energetic Drum Major who I knew would go down well in Edinburgh. We then sent off for the 300-mile trip north to the Khyber in convoy. I did persuade them to turn off the sirens.

We stopped overnight at the grand old British Peshawar GHQ Officers' Mess where I was given a suite of rooms and three dedicated staff.

'What do I do with them,' I thought. *'Such luxury?'*

So, one pressed my creased uniform and suits, one cleaned my shoes and the last brought me food and more Coca-Cola. They were charming and I wanted to bring them home. The following morning, I had a chance to walk around the centre of Peshawar and found the Grand Bazaar to be a truly impressive market. I was searching for Kilim carpets and there were thousands. In the end, I bought four quality carpets in Islamabad with the help and expertise of the Defence Adviser.

That day, we entered the Khyber Pass through the magnificent Khyber Gate and as we did so the Military Police Jeep was replaced by an armoured truck with a pintle-mounted machine gun.

I asked, 'Why the gun?'

Shabbir replied, 'You just can't trust the Tribes.'

To me, they appeared perfectly friendly. What was far more dangerous was our drive up the pass at speed, overtaking. We spent most of the time on the wrong side of the road with a mass of large trucks from Afghanistan hurtling towards us. There were trucks, buses and carts drawn by horses, mules and donkeys, all decked out in glorious technicolour making their way up and down the pass. On each side of the road, there were tiny villages all fortified by mud walls and on top of the hills, military forts and outposts as tribal war still goes on as it has done for hundreds of years when the British Raj and the Indian Army tried and failed to bring peace to the area. The British Regiments serving there in those days have left their mark with the cap badges of great regiments such as The Black Watch, etched into the rock of the pass.

The pass was surrounded by beautiful country and on the east side of the road against the hills is the extraordinary Khyber Railway clinging to the cliffs on viaducts and through tunnels climbing up the pass to Landi Kōtal at 3,500 ft. It was only completed in 1935 by Victor Bailey, a talented British Army engineer, who it appears, without a deserved accolade, created this remarkable feat of architecture and engineering.

First, we drove to the border overlooking Afghanistan for a briefing from an Army outpost. Little did I know that British troops would again be operationally involved here just four years later.

Landi Kōtal fort is the barracks and home of the Khyber Rifles raised by the British Raj in 1880 to guard the North West Frontier. I had an appointment to meet the Commander, Colonel Malik Naeem Ullah Khan, and to witness a display of Khattak dancers from the regiment. On arrival, I was given a seat in a traditional Officers' Mess leather armchair, in the garden, all by myself, and attended by three smart Military Staff and served good old-fashioned tea. After some time, the Commander arrived looking somewhat dishevelled and frustrated.

I rose to meet him, offering the normal Pakistan greeting, 'Salam.'

And he said to me, 'My dear Brigadier so sorry I'm late – trouble with the Tribes.'

I thought that this very statement was one that could have been said many times over hundreds of years by his forebears. He had just returned from operations in the mountains.

We watched various displays by the colourful Regimental Khattak dancers – so professional and Dervish in style – a must for The Tattoo. We then went for lunch in the Officers' Mess, which was world famous because of visits by visiting heads of state and the international 'great and the good' over many years: The Queen, the Shah of Persia, President Kennedy, Princess Diana, Winston Churchill, Sean Connery and many more who all left their photographs in the anteroom, they did not ask for mine!

We had a delicious lunch. There were more servants than officers. There was even a small band seated on cushions on the floor playing gentle Khyber music.

After another unforgettable day, we had to return to Rawalpindi. Our trip down the Pass was swift, back to Islamabad where I was accommodated in the Armoured Corps Officers' Mess.

The next day was my last. I was invited to the Independence Parade in Islamabad – the 50th Anniversary – which was attended by Islamic heads of state. A massive and most impressive parade of thousands from the Army, Navy and Air Force and the elegant and colourful mounted President's Bodyguard (formerly the Viceroy's Bodyguard) – finely-drilled, disciplined, marching troops, splendid in their grand and colourful uniforms. It was a magnificent performance and ended with a flypast about the size of our present Royal Air Force. I was then generously bid farewell at dinner by the DGPS, Major General Jamshed Ayaz Khan, who presented me with a briefcase that I still use to this day.

My BA return flight was early (7.30 am) and at 6.30 am the whole airport was buzzing with people heading for London; families, grannies, children, trunks, animals, and it was somewhat challenging fighting though the crowds to get to the BA Business Class desk. Eventually, the BA lady informed me my luggage was overweight (I thought, *'Oh no, it is The Kilim Carpets'*), but then she asked if I would like to be upgraded to First Class. So without further ado, I sat down in sumptuous luxury in BA's wonderful Jumbo Jet first-class cabin feeling very much 'at home' at last. At 7 am, just prior to take off, an air hostess offered me a drink of either water, orange juice or champagne.

So, after seven dry days, I had a delicious glass of vintage Krug or two. I thought, *'What a suitable conclusion to my long travels.'*

On returning to Edinburgh, I felt so much more confident about being able to deliver to our huge audiences some special international guests which most people would otherwise never see.

The 1997 show was blessed with a most talented Senior Director of Music, the late Lieutenant Colonel Richard Waterer, OBE, RM, and his three high-quality Royal Marine Bands together with a Massed Pipes and Drums of ten bands. I had also asked for a Royal Marines team from Comacchio Group RM (Commandos who guard the submarine nuclear facility at HNNB Faslane on the west coast of Scotland) to give us a dynamic action display, abseiling down Edinburgh Castle and impressively destroying a band of terrorists.

Our 50 Highland dancers, under the direction of Billy Forsyth, MBE, gave us 'The Ceilidh Dance' dressed in a more contemporary manner: short skirts! This was the first of our tightly choreographed Massed Highland Dancing and it was fast-moving and brilliant. Furthermore, it set a new standard which was then emulated by many other international Tattoos.

Our overseas guests added so much fun to The Tattoo: Pakistan's Pipe Band and the Dervish Khattak dancers; the Trinidad and Tobago Defence Force Steel Band took the audience by storm. We also welcomed back our friends, the Lochiel Marching Team.

The finale included the tune 'Gael' ('Last of the Mohicans'), a new arrangement for Pipes and Band by Warrant Officer 1 Matt MacDermott and the original 'Amazing Grace' all of which the audience loved.

The Tattoo was now selling 85 per cent of its tickets, we would soon make that 100 per cent.

During the last two years, I had still been serving in the Army, commanding 51 Highland Brigade as well as being the producer of The Tattoo – unpaid! So life had been a touch hectic. The Board of Directors then invited me to take on the official appointment of CEO and Producer; by this time, I was hooked by The Tattoo, so I resigned my commission early after 33 years.

CHAPTER 4
1998

IN 1998, having left the Army, as CEO, I now had to run the company business and the production, so life became more challenging. On the retirement of the extremely competent business manager, Brian Leishman, I found and appointed Lieutenant Colonel Richard Hamblelton, TD, as my financial director. I had met Richard when he was in command of The Scottish Transport Regiment. He was passionate about The Tattoo. During his TA life, he had been part of the old lighting team but he came to us as a successful senior civil servant in the Scottish Government.

Richard was crucial to The Tattoo's success: he dealt very efficiently with all the essential administrative, financial and business matters, the 'nitty gritty', leaving me free to concentrate on the show, but he had an annoying knack of controlling my extravagant ideas!

Richard, due to his previous experience, was also in charge of lighting design, which was essential in creating the desired atmosphere and the 'Son et Lumiere' on the much-admired Edinburgh Castle. Sound and light were an indispensable part of the full panoply of The Tattoo and I was lucky to inherit our sound designer from my predecessor, John Del Nero, whose experience and expertise were internationally renowned. He was passionate about the show and with his team, for some 30 years, provided us with an excellent sound design and a cutting-edge sound system.

This year, we had the pleasure of The Coldstream Guards under the direction of Major David Marshall, a skilled Director of Music, and eleven Pipes and Drums including our special guests from New Zealand, the Pipes and Drums of Invercargill and Dunedin. I asked David Marshall if he would please arrange 'Hector the Hero', a tune which was suggested by my two sons Harry and Michael. I first heard it in the kitchen at home, they played me the tune by Wolfstone as a potential combined number and they were right. David, after some deliberation and with great talent, produced a fantastic arrangement for Massed Pipes and Military Bands and it was one of the best finale numbers ever. It can be found on YouTube.

I had some travelling to do to check our Acts for this year, 1998, and find new ones for the future.

Many of us are fascinated by Russia – *War and Peace*, 1812, the beautiful St Petersburg, the sensational film *Dr Zhivago*, the horrific demise of Tsar Nicholas and the Russian royal family and much more. Having lived through the Cold War with my regiment based in West Germany with the British Army of The Rhine (BAOR), I badly wanted to visit. I had heard that the quality of their bands and cultural acts was very high and just ten years after the Cold War an invitation to them was not before time. At a meeting in 1997, I had been asked by a Russian, Vitaly Mironov, to come to Moscow. He was offering the Central Band of The Russian Navy. We were short of an act for 1998, so I set off to Moscow and like Washington, I stayed in one of their finest hotels, *The Baltschug Kempinski*, the first five-star hotel to be opened after the Soviet era with a wonderful view of the Kremlin and its beautiful golden-domed cathedrals.

It was February and, therefore, it was not surprising that the temperature in Moscow was minus 30 degrees and covered in snow and ice. The first morning, I was shown around the Kremlin by Dr Dmitry Fedosov whose knowledge of Scottish and Russian history was unsurpassed. His father had been deputy ambassador to Britain during the Cold War. Dmitry said I needed a hat as the temperature was so low I would get a headache, so I bought a wonderful black rabbit fur hat from a stall – it looked just like mink! I was given a fascinating tour of the stunning cathedrals; there are four left inside the Kremlin including the Assumption Cathedral where Tsars were crowned, the Archangel Cathedral where they were buried, and the Annunciation Cathedral used by the Tsars and family as a private chapel. I was then taken to the main museum, the Kremlin Armoury, and beside it, the Diamond Fund, where there are a few of the main Tsarist diamond treasures left, which are just sensational. I was surprised that they had survived the Soviet era.

By 3 pm, we had not had lunch. This, in true classic Russian style, turned out to be a bottle of vodka and a long afternoon. Later, we had an excellent dinner in a Georgian restaurant with fine Georgian wine – after all this generous hospitality I amazingly survived unscathed.

The following day, we visited the Central Band of the Russian Navy which gave an impressive display with familiar tunes such as 'Kalinka' and 'Moscow Nights'. I was most impressed. I asked for singing and dancing to be included in the act for Edinburgh and, importantly, the entrancing balalaika.

That night, there was a traditional Russian dinner in a restaurant. There was not much food but a succession of toasts - Russia, Scotland, The Queen, of course, Tsar Nicholas, the Regiment and, yes, even the wives and much more. Each toast was thrown back with vodka - it went on for some time.

I was, therefore, very pleased to easily navigate my way to my hotel room safely and considering everything, I felt rather well. However, this did not last long and when I awoke the next morning I thought I was going to die. That morning, I had scheduled a meeting with the Defence Attaché. I rang to say I had become rather busy. He replied, 'So you had a good night?'; you could say, lesson learned.

The Central Navy Band would come free and flights covered, so as usual we would just fund food and accommodation - a good deal and it would be the first appearance of Russia at The Tattoo.

I am forever grateful to Vitaly and Dmitry for my introduction to Russia and the impressive military music and culture that they presented to me. This was the first of many visits.

In March, it was time for my next world tour, this time to check on already invited acts and also to find new ones.

I flew to Australia first, with BA in business class which was, as ever, very comfortable. At that time, their international service was second to none; thirteen hours to Singapore and twelve on to Sydney and thence to the capital, Canberra. Canberra is relatively new as a capital city, formed in 1913 and completed in 1927. I was keen to secure Australian military involvement in the show.

I was invited to stay with my good friend, Colonel Mark Radford, 16th/5th Lancers, who was Assistant Defence Adviser. He had a charming house in the country and the garden was inhabited by a herd of kangaroos. On arrival, I was given a fascinating tour of the new Parliament Building, the architect designed it to be inside 'Capitol Hill' with a massive mast and flag. The approaches and roof are covered in grass, so that 'the people' can walk all over the roof, and indeed their politicians! Visible $1^{1}/_{4}$ miles away along Anzac Parade is the most important landmark in Australia - the magnificent War Memorial where every fatal Australian military casualty is recorded.

At dinner that night, I met the Chief of The Army, Lieutenant General Sanderson, and an old friend, General John Coates, who years before had commanded a squadron of The Royal Scots Greys in Germany, Lieutenant Colonel John Stanier who became a Field Marshal and head of the British Army. John Coates successfully retired as Chief of the Australian Army.

The next day, the Defence Attaché arranged a meeting with the Senior Director of Music to discuss possible involvement but, sadly, with the Olympic Games coming up there was not huge enthusiasm at that time. We came together later in 2005 for our Tattoo in Sydney.

After a short catch-up in New Zealand, and taking the advice of the Defence Attaché, my next stop was the Cook Islands – easier said than done as it is about as far away as you can get in the South Pacific, 2,000 miles from Auckland and 4,000 miles from Los Angeles but comfortable Air New Zealand drops in en route to LA from Auckland, a trip of four hours. I left on 17 March and arrived on 16 March as we crossed the dateline; I got an extra day in the South Pacific.

The Cook Islands are one of the most beautiful groups of islands in the whole world, spread over nearly a million square miles consisting of fifteen islands with a total population of only 18,000. The capital is Avarua on the largest island Rarotonga, which has a population of 9,000 people, a circumference of 20 miles with its own mountain, Rua Manga, standing at 2,000 ft.

Arriving at Rarotonga is an experience in itself. On approach, we flew over a wonderful turquoise lagoon and you get the impression that you are landing in paradise – and indeed you are! The runway runs parallel to the white sandy beach and a tiny palm-fronded terminal building. I was greeted by a charming Cook Islander, Papatua Papatua, who was to be my guide for the visit, and presented with garlands of stephanotis and jasmine – certainly beats Heathrow. Papatua was a huge help and became a great friend. Everyone on the island knew him as he was a champion dancer in his day and a most popular figure. I intended to check out Polynesian dancing troupes with a view to an invitation for 2001. I was accommodated at the Edgewater Resort and on the beach – my room was almost in the surf.

That night, we witnessed the first cabaret at the Edgewater Resort – one of the many dancing troupes on the island – unspoilt by tourism and brilliant. Strong tribal dancing by the boys and, in contrast, elegant girls with flowers in their long black hair, coconut tops and just a grass skirt, all accompanied by traditional music with guitar and vibrant drumming.

I asked Papatua boldly, 'When did the girls start wearing those fetching coconut tops?'

He said, 'When you sent the missionaries in 1820.' And added, 'The missionaries were actually quite happy with the girls running around topless but when their wives arrived to join them later, they said to their missionary husbands, "Darling you can't have young women running around with nothing on".'

The next day, I was taken to meet The Queen's Representative on the Island, HE Mr Frederick Goodwin (ranking as the Governor), in his charming bungalow with a large, polished brass plate on the gate on which was the crown of Her Majesty The Queen. He was dressed elegantly in a suit and I was invited to have tea on the veranda looking out over the bay.

He was a man of few words and there was a long pause in the conversation so I said, 'How's tourism on the island?'

He replied gruffly, 'We have quite enough. Your missionaries told us to dress up and go to church on Sunday which we all still do, wearing a suit and the women a dress and hat, but if you look out on the lagoon in front of my house on Sunday, you will find English women lying there wearing nothing at all.'

I saw a total of three dancing groups and extended an invitation for 2001. They were all so impressive so it was decided to form a joint group from the schools, a total of 58 and I was to come back and see them next year in rehearsals. I met the Minister of Tourism who arranged for me to see the Prime Minister. That night, I was invited to the only nightclub on the island and at midnight there was a dancing display. Thanks to Papatua, a welcoming announcement came over the microphone:

'Tonight, we welcome Mel Jameson, the producer of the world-famous Edinburgh Tattoo, and he is going to dance with – Miss South Pacific.'

There was nowhere to hide.

The following day, I was sent on a tour of the cultural village which was cleverly put together for visitors and they spoke about the history and culture of the island.

They also said, 'We used to be British [since 1888] then, in 1965, we were surprised to be told by the British Foreign Secretary to grow up and be independent, when we were in fact quite happy – and at our Independence Day, they did not even send a Royal to cut the ribbon.'

There was clearly some unhappiness, so they decided to change the flag, which is similar to that of Australia and New Zealand with the Union Flag, to a plain green one without the Union Flag. However, no one liked it so they eventually kept the old one. Interestingly, they all very well remember with fondness the arrival of HMS *Britannia* in 1974 and the visit by The Queen and Prince Philip. The islands are now happy and administered by New Zealand.

I flew back to Auckland and, by crossing the date line, I again lost a day of my life!

I visited Fiji once more to tie up the final details of their performance and see a rehearsal. I was invited to a meeting at Queen Elizabeth Barracks, chaired by the charming and welcoming Captain Frank Bainimarama of the Fiji Navy. He was later appointed Chief of Armed Forces Fiji and retired as a Rear Admiral. In 2000 and 2006, he instigated bloodless coups against what was described as corrupt regimes and Prime Ministers, and Fiji was sadly suspended from The Commonwealth temporarily. Captain Bainimarama eventually established a new regime and was credited with introducing more ethnic diversity. He is now in his second term as Prime Minister of Fiji.

I was particularly honoured with a wonderful five-course lunch in the Officers' Mess – they like their food in Fiji – before which I had to sing for my supper with a briefing about The Tattoo.

After lunch, I witnessed a dress rehearsal of the act with 40 Bandsmen in full uniform and twenty warriors in grass skirts. It was a great act, which concluded with the emotional Fiji song 'Leaving the Island – Isa Lei'.

The act from Fiji at The 1998 Tattoo was a triumph and footage from the show can still be easily found on YouTube – it was excellent. During August that year, the warriors, fit and true, said they wanted to join the British Army. I knew that Fijians had served in the Army before as we had a superb and universally popular gentleman in The Scots Greys, Sergeant Shute. We took them to the recruiting office in Queen Street, Edinburgh. All eighteen passed the tests and were sworn in but they had to return to Fiji first to sign off.

CHAPTER 4 - 1998

Later that week, I spoke to our Chief of the General Staff attending the Tattoo. The British Army, as ever, was seriously short of recruits. I told him about my new eighteen recruits and I said, 'Why don't you recruit across The Commonwealth for volunteers?'

He laughed at my suggestion, not realising about the imminent Fiji invasion of recruits. Six months later, when Fijians heard the news of the warriors, they all wanted to join up. The MOD had to put a cap on Fiji recruits at 2,500. Since that year, 1998, they have proved to be brave and professional soldiers through all the recent challenging operational campaigns, in Iraq and Afghanistan in particular.

It was sad to leave Fiji again but good to be on the way home – via Los Angeles, ten hours, to JFK New York, five hours, and then down to Barbados for my last stop of four hours. Barbados were now confirmed for 1999 and a year later their act was excellent and ready to go.

For 1998, we had no theme and no one seemed to notice. We did have more overseas acts, however, including Fiji, and for the first time, a Russian Act – the Russian Navy Central Band – as well as Irish Celtic dancers and the ever popular Honda Imps Motorcycle Display Team. Now called the Imps Motorcycle Display Team, they were started 52 years ago by Roy Pratt, MBE. Roy deserves an accolade for producing such a thrilling act and inspiring hundreds of deprived children from East London.

The strength of the Massed Pipes and Drums of eleven bands was magnificent with our friends from Dunedin and Invercargill, who themselves did a remarkable solo act, coming down the esplanade playing reels on the march including 'Itchy Fingers' and 'Clumsy Lover' and finishing with 'Pōkarekare Ana'.

The Military Band, led by The Coldstream Guards, surpassed themselves and included that great march 'Grandioso' and then in the finale with Massed Combined Bands (Military Bands and Pipes and Drums) we had David Marshall's spectacular arrangement of 'Hector The Hero'. For me, it was outstanding and went down so well with the audience. It has since been emulated across the world by many tattoos.

CHAPTER 5
1999

IN 1999, THE TATTOO celebrated half a century, having been created in 1950. I invited the Military Bands of The Royal Armoured Corps to celebrate this occasion (what was left of them after defence cuts), The Mounted Band of the Life Guards, the Bands of The Dragoon Guards, the Hussars and Light Dragoons, The Royal Lancers and The Royal Tank Regiment. A decade later, there would be only one band left. We also had the privilege of featuring the Drum Horses from the Life Guards, The Royal Scots Dragoon Guards and The Queens Royal Hussars. The Massed Pipes and Drums included the excellent Vancouver Police Pipes and Drums.

Travel throughout this year for me was extensive. In January, I visited India for a week and on return to Heathrow, after the ten-hour flight, I had to change planes for Boston. In March, I visited Berlin for the International Trade Fair and the USA again to meet a University/College Band. In May, I flew back to New Zealand and, finally in November, I was Down Under again.

The visit to India was of particular interest as my father had spent so much time there serving with the Indian Army (the Punjabis) and later as a tea planter in Assam. My father greatly enjoyed his military service with the Indian Army after the horrors of the First World War. He was a very competent horseman and he had access to many horse activities including polo and pig sticking. After about fifteen years in India, he met my mother when he was home on leave and soon became engaged. Then in 1935, they were married in St Andrews Church, Calcutta, and had a happy two years in Assam before returning home.

En route to India, I was reading up on India's history. I remember being rather appalled reading *Freedom At Midnight* by Larry Collins and Dominique Lapierre which rather triumphed over 'Partition' and the way they had handed over India in such short order, which was largely due to Labour Government pressure and resulted in the formation of India and Pakistan, as opposed to one country complete within The Commonwealth – this, as history relates, caused a multitude of never-ending conflict and wars.

This visit was to New Delhi: I had been invited by the Defence Adviser, Brigadier SMA Lee, to the two big annual events in India, The Republic Day Parade and The Beating Retreat. My mission was to find an Indian act for the 2000 Tattoo Commonwealth celebration. I stayed in one of the very best hotels in India, *The Oberoi*. The Oberoi Group, the most exclusive hotel chain in India, was owned by Mr P R S (Biki) Oberoi, who I knew from my time as Chairman of Army Polo at home. He had generously sponsored the Indian Polo team for the match at Windsor against the British Army in 1990 and presented the silver prizes made by Asprey.

Later that week, I was invited to his farm outside Delhi to meet him again and, over a large whisky, he agreed to ask the Indian Foreign Minister to support my plan for a band or act.

The Republic Day parade followed for which there was heavy security along the impressive Raj Path – no telephones, cameras or bags. The format for the three-hour parade was similar to the one I had witnessed in Islamabad but bigger and grander – thousands of highly disciplined well-drilled marching troops and Military Bands in brilliant ceremonial uniform, Pipes and Drums and Mounted Bands, in particular the President's Bodyguard in the old Viceroy's elegant uniform of scarlet and gold and the wonderful 61st Cavalry from Jaipur in blue and yellow. And yes, there were magnificent, gracious and heavily-decorated elephants. There followed military equipment of all sorts including the Agni (nuclear) missile and an impressive flypast led by the Chief of the Air Staff who they said was back in his VIP seat by the end of the parade! Then a nice contrast, cultural dancers with children from across India and floats. However, I thought that the musical stars of the show were the Border Security Force Mounted Camel Band dressed in orange uniform and turban – they played better than anyone and looked spectacular. This was a must for The Tattoo so I was determined to pay them a visit. Notably, the parade's attendees included the President and Prime Minister and their guest, the King of Nepal.

This visit to India was an important first look and as we learnt in the cavalry, 'Time spent in reconnaissance is seldom wasted'. At the end of the week, as I was so keen on the Border Security Force Camel Band, the Defence Advisor arranged an interview for me with the Director General who was charming and enthusiastic. I invited the band knowing it would have to be sea travel and expensive – he, without any hesitation, said, 'Yes'.

Camels on the esplanade was a perfect Tattoo act. However, on my return to Scotland, I asked the relevant ministry department in London for guidance. They informed me that EU regulations and protocol banned any importation of camels into Europe – no chance at all, so sadly that was that.

On my next visit to India, I looked at different options.

I arrived at Heathrow from India, changed planes and flew directly to Boston for the Scottish Tourist Board marketing tour of the States, the aim of which was to market key activities in Scotland and increase, or at least maintain, the number of tourists from the USA. For example, The Tattoo was already welcoming 20,000 people each year from the USA so the aim was to increase that if possible. The programme was hectic but a great opportunity to see the USA. It was in fact an exhausting 'Ten Cities in Ten days' programme including Long Island, Newark, Baltimore, Dallas, LA, San Francisco, Phoenix, Chicago and Detroit.

I was interested in visiting Boston having heard so much about it and I was told it was an Anglified city. That said, I did not detect much love for the British – probably because of the many Irish immigrants, mainly caused by poverty and the Great Famine in the mid-nineteenth century (22 per cent of the population claim Irish heritage). I had a spare day so I took a bus trip around the city and, as we approached the harbour, the conductor asked the passengers where they came from.

'Anyone from England?' he asked.

So being Scottish/British I said nothing. He then proceeded to lambast the English/British for every sort of thing not least the Boston Tea Party!

Two stops later, I could take no more and as I left the bus, I said to the conductor, 'I am proud to be Scottish and British, I have found your words ignorant and offensive.'

I think he was quite surprised.

The daily routine following an American breakfast was the opportunity to give our own individual presentations to the Travel trade people – about a hundred of them – for two hours and then, with only a small lunch, we caught a plane for the next venue. I found it a useful and well-organised operation but later handed it over to my excellent marketing and publicity manager, Alan Smith, as my programme was getting frenetic.

In May, I had to visit the USA again, albeit briefly. I flew to St Louis via Chicago to visit the University of Missouri which I was told had a spectacular College Band. There, I was met by Dr Barry Bernhardt who drove me to Cape Girardeau and the University of Missouri which is situated by the banks of the mighty Mississippi River. The College Band with its amazing drum line looked perfect for The Tattoo and if nothing else would be a huge contrast from the norm, albeit rather contemporary; and like all American College Bands they moved and played fast, changing tunes and formations almost at the run so I attempted to slow them down a bit so we could hear those great American numbers like 'St Louis Blues', 'Battle Hymn of the Republic' and 'Yankee Doodle'.

On my way home, I checked out Barbados again to attend a final rehearsal and thankfully the band played well. What made the act particularly special was the carnival performers in wonderful costumes and the Moco Jumbie stilts walkers – what an improvement!

On my way to Barbados from Miami, I met a charming person sitting beside me in the front of business class and, unusually in an aircraft, we chatted. He asked where I came from and I told him Perthshire in Scotland.

He paused and said, 'I have just got engaged to the former wife of Captain David Gemmell.' David was a very good friend and close neighbour of mine – a small world and a coincidence indeed. My new acquaintance was Cow Williams the renowned landowner of Barbados, who owned herds of cattle, building works and hill estates. He was also the inspiration and organiser of polo on the island.

The next day, he kindly showed me around the island – in his Range Rover – which is very beautiful, and pointed out his many interests and properties. I was later told that it is possible to walk from one end of the island to the other on land owned by Sir Cow Williams; he was recently knighted in The Queen's Birthday Honours. New Zealand would be my next stop.

The Royal Edinburgh Military Tattoo had been invited by the New Zealand Festival of Arts to perform in Wellington in 2000. My initial reaction was that it was too difficult and time-consuming. Never before had The Tattoo in its full glory performed abroad – a potential logistic nightmare. However, we eventually agreed, saying that we would accept the invitation as long as we could bring Edinburgh Castle!

Consequently, I was bidden to New Zealand for an important recce and to meet the New Zealand team, see the arena and talk about the programme and production for 2000 and the contract.

CHAPTER 5 - 1999

So, back to Windy Wellington to meet the team including the CEO of the New Zealand Festival, Carla Van Zon, and the production executive, Alex Reedijk. After the long flight of 30 hours from Edinburgh via London, Singapore and Auckland, I arrived in Wellington feeling a touch jetlagged and much looking forward to some rest in my hotel. The CEO met me at the airport. 'We are first off to a press conference,' she said brightly, as if I had popped in from next door. 'They are waiting for us and will be expecting a full brief from you on The Tattoo!'

They took me to see the brand new, and still under construction Westpac Stadium locally known as 'The Cake Tin' as it is completely round and built entirely for cricket and rugby. What else would one expect in New Zealand. It would take 34,000 but with a castle set in place, seating would be restricted to a mere 20,000 - they had agreed to build Edinburgh Castle in the arena and promised a decent replica. I was content with all the plans and confident we would manage, but we would need a larger cast to fill this huge arena. (The full story is covered in the next chapter.)

I was dining again with the Defence Adviser that evening so I thought I had better bring a present. I stopped the taxi in central Wellington and as I was late, I ran up the street, not knowing where the booze shop was; I saw a local leaning against the wall, rather out of breath.

'Can you tell me where I can quickly get some whisky?' I asked.

'Sure, Mate, just up there on the left,' he replied.

Thus off I went at the run.

On my way back, I passed the local again.

'I hope you are feeling better now, Mate,' he proffered.

And so 1999 was a success. The Mounted Band of the Life Guards looked most impressive with the magnificent drum horses of the cavalry and the other Dismounted Bands. After all my visits, we at last presented the Barbados Military Band who did very well in their unique suave uniforms; and the stilt walkers so tall they were able to look the audience in the eye and every night tossed flowers into the stands. Our other visitors, the Golden Eagles College Band, represented the USA in style, marching down the arena to the 'Battle Hymn' and other well-known tunes - 'Sing Sing Sing' and 'Yankee Doodle Dandy' - while their drum line added a young and contemporary touch.

CHAPTER 6
2000

THE YEAR 2000 was to be the busiest and biggest so far with three major events: The Royal Edinburgh Military Tattoo in New Zealand in March, a special tribute to The Queen Mother on her 100th birthday in July and The 50th Anniversary Tattoo in Edinburgh in August. The first and biggest challenge in 2000 was The New Zealand Tattoo.

There was huge enthusiasm in New Zealand to bring The Tattoo to Wellington. This was largely due to the fact that, like Australia, many watch BBC World 'The Royal Edinburgh Military Tattoo' after The Queen's Speech on Christmas Day. Our initial thoughts were as to whether we needed this challenge. However, the promise of raising more money for Service charities was encouraging and it was an exciting prospect to take The Tattoo overseas for the first time and, even better, 'Down Under'.

Following the first meeting in Edinburgh with Carla Van Zon, the CEO and artistic director of the New Zealand Festival, Wellington – an emulation of the Edinburgh International Festival and a charity – our thoughts were that if we both make a decent surplus then it would go to both charities rather than the personal pocket of an impresario. The plan was that The Tattoo would take place in an outdoor arena, the Westpac Stadium, in Wellington, over three nights. It would be organised, administered and promoted by the New Zealand Festival and, importantly, they would 'take the risk' to protect the interests of 'Edinburgh Military Tattoo Charities'. Regarding Edinburgh Castle, this presented them with a small challenge. They were, nonetheless, undaunted and the extraordinary replica of the frontage of the Castle, was accurate in every detail and was central to our success Down Under. The show took place in March on the advice of the local team as they said that it never rains in Wellington during March.

We took our full production team to New Zealand including:

Richard Hambleton General Manager and Lighting.
Steve Walsh Production Manager.
Colonel Alasdair Hutton Narrator.

Lieutenant Colonel Waterer, Royal Marines Senior Director of Music.
Major Gavin Stoddart Director of Army Bagpipe Music.
Lieutenant Colonel David Price Musical Adviser.
Billy Forsyth Highland Dancing Director.
Major Jamie Erskine Commander Troops.

The arena was much larger than Edinburgh so I had to ensure a suitably large cast but there were restrictions on numbers.

By now, after many visits to New Zealand, I was aware of the talent that they could provide so, with the help of the New Zealand Ministry of Defence and the chairman of the New Zealand Pipes and Drums Association, my plan was for a cast of a thousand:

Massed Pipes and Drums Six from home and seven from
   New Zealand; thirteen bands (each of twenty) – 260 musicians.
Military Bands We were lucky to get The Royal Marines,
   Scots Guards and the Highland and Lowland Bands, and from
   New Zealand the brilliant New Zealand Army Band, the Navy and
   the Royal New Zealand Air Force Band – 210 musicians in all.
Highland Dancers Scottish and New Zealand dancers – 200 dancers.
Maori Kapa Haka
The Lochiel Marching Team Veterans of The Tattoo in Edinburgh.
Fiji Our friends from Fiji, their band and warriors, who had
   performed in Edinburgh in 1998.

The New Zealand Festival had planned for three nights but as the tickets went on sale, it was very quickly 'sold out' so we agreed to perform for a fourth night – our free night off. So 80,000 would watch our show!

This news concentrated the mind and we now had to live up to New Zealand's expectations.

We had a great cast with a huge Massed Pipes and Drums and the best Military Bands so we needed to select lots of impressive stirring music which the audience would enjoy. This aspect is far more important than some people realise. The aim, particularly in the finale, is to make people in the audience feel happy, perhaps emotional and certainly proud of their country.

Our rehearsals over three days started at Trentham Army Camp just outside Wellington, where the cast was accommodated. Then we moved to the 'Cake Tin' arena which presented plenty of challenges not planned for, such as lighting because of the round arena and sound issues.

The first night went like a dream. What a relief. In the finale with the Pipes and Bands, we played that great Maori tune 'Pōkarekare Anna' sung by the talented Joanna Heslop followed by 'Highland Cathedral' which is also loved in New Zealand. The evening hymn was 'Now is the Hour' and after two of our great national anthems, 'Old Lang Syne'.

The narrator, Alasdair Hutton, did a fine job as ever and then came to the announcement for the lone piper (who happened to be Pipe Major Bruce Hitchings who had joined the Gordon Highlanders and the British Army as a young man from New Zealand).

Alasdair announced, 'The lone piper tonight is Pipe Major Bruce Hitchings, the Senior Pipe Major of the British Army, from Palmerston North (Wellington).'

There followed a roar of appreciation from the entire audience.

We came to the last night – warm balmy weather, a perfect evening. However, as we approached the finale there was a rush of wind and rain as the whole cast marched on to 'Bonnie Lass of Fyvie'. Then, as they were playing 'Pōkarekare Anna', down came torrential rain, driven into the arena by storm force winds; the lighting structure was swinging dangerously, the Castle was being torn apart and the arena was unsafe. How could we end the show with no communication with the Director of Music who was at the other end of the arena?

I said to Alasdair, 'How do we stop this?'

He said to leave it to him and as the bands finished the first number of the long finale, he announced, 'In view of the weather we will end the show with "Scotland the Brave"' (The march-off tune).'

Luckily, despite the noise of wind and rain, when the baton came down, the musicians all hit the right note and executed the march-off. It was, nonetheless, a tense moment. So much for, 'It never rains in Wellington in March'.

It was a great privilege and pleasure to perform in Wellington and a triumph for the excellent cast who were leaving for home overnight and the next day with very wet uniforms. Without a doubt, the show was a huge success, the crowd appeared to love it, we made a good surplus for Tri-Service charities and it enhanced our great relationship with

New Zealand and The Commonwealth.

After a pause at home, in May I had to travel overseas to visit some new acts to keep the momentum going and check out some for the approaching Tattoo.

I found South Africa completely fascinating with its stunning countryside. This was my second visit. I started in Durban and was taken by the Natal Militia in an Army Land Rover on an amazing visit to the old battlefields of Rorke's Drift and Isandlwana where a British Army detachment of 1,750 was defeated and wiped out by the Zulu Army. The film *Zulu* only features the second part of the day, Rorke's Drift, which was indeed a victory but a very expensive one with eleven VCs awarded.

On this visit, I found that there were many potential acts for The Tattoo which had never been seen in Britain before. A well-kept secret was their military Pipes and Drums in their militia and regular regiments; there were about six including the Witwatersrand Rifles (affiliated to the Cameronians), the Transvaal Scots (affiliated to The Black Watch) and the Cape Town Highlanders (affiliated to the Gordon Highlanders) who became regular attenders in Edinburgh.

My visit started with Defence Force HQ in Pretoria where I met a number of generals including the Chief of Personnel and the Chief of Human Resources who appeared very supportive and this would help with the future provision of bands and acts from the South African military.

Then I was off to visit the Zulu Battalion of the South African Army at Mtubatuba, Kwa Zulu-Natal, 200 miles north of Durban – an extraordinary experience. I felt like the South Wales Borderers at Rorke's Drift surrounded by 1,000 Zulus.

We put together a display with slapping shields and chanting from the film *Zulu* and the charge followed at the end by the battle song. I was quite pleased with the plan. However, when they arrived several months later in Edinburgh, my plot had all been completely forgotten. Indeed, I think they were a completely different set of Zulus, so, in desperation, we built a small sangar on the esplanade with British soldiers in scarlet and white helmets, as in the film *Rorke's Drift*, and the Zulus suddenly became enthusiastic. They did a fierce war dance which was extremely scary, then, with their spears, charged the soldiers in white helmets. The soldiers were supposed to be brave, stand and pretend to fight, but in sheer terror, they fell and died before the Zulus got there.

I left for Cape Town and various meetings all day but importantly I had the pleasure of meeting the Cape Town Highlanders and the very competent Pipe Major Charles Canning.

That evening, I was invited to dinner at Cape Castle, the home of the Cape Town Highlanders, and this was an experience in itself. The evening was an extravaganza of music and a fascinating programme:

> *The Christmas Band* At the gateway to the Castle was what was known as a Christmas Band. The band is drawn from the black community and is mainly brass playing hymns. The band is dressed in suits and bowler hats – a great sound and a nice surprise.
> *The Minstrels* After arrival at the Officers' Mess, we watched from the balcony as the Minstrels performed in the Castle courtyard. They are from the Asian community of Cape Town; playing Dixie Jazz, dressed in bright blazers and boaters and brass, drums and banjos – full of fun and pizazz.

We sat down for a smart mess dinner. I noticed on the wall of the dining room portraits of various royals – Queen Victoria, King George V and VI and Queen Elizabeth The Queen Mother, their Colonel-in-Chief. I was told that she secretly remained fully active during the apartheid period of government. We drank her health at the end of dinner.

Then two more bands:

> *Moslem Pipes and Drums* Dressed in fez and baggy trousers and spats – an interesting sound.
> *Drums and Pipes of the Cape Town Highlanders* A great performance from this quality band. They could not have been any better than the Pipes and Drums from Scotland's Regiments. (For interest the title 'Drums and Pipes' is used otherwise only by the Gordon Highlanders.)

In short, a most memorable evening, an extravaganza of South African Music – what could be better?

The following morning, I flew to Adelaide, a stunning city with the best climate in Australia and the best wine. It was a twelve-hour flight and I arrived slightly jaded, looking forward to a peaceful night to recover but little chance of that as a full evening programme had been organised including a formal visit to the Lord Mayor and an official welcoming dinner.

I asked my new friend and guide as to whether I had time to book into my hotel and get changed as I intended to meet some new bands and some I had met on my previous visit:

10/27 Battalion, The Royal Australian Regiment. My first visit to this reserve regiment with a small band dressed in the colonial style; white tunic and white traditional helmet.

They gave a joint band display including the excellent *South Australia Police Band* and the *Pipes and Drums of Adelaide University.*

I invited them all to The Tattoo over the next few years but the South Australia Police would perform this year, 2000, at our Golden Anniversary show along with an Aboriginal group.

I was collected at 5 am by Chief Inspector John Fitzgerald who whisked me to the airport in his police car. I was bound for the Cooks again for I had to finalise their visit for 2001.

This was a more challenging visit as I had to persuade the hierarchy that sending 58 young people across the world to what was considered to be a wet and cold Scotland was a good idea. Meetings were arranged with the Minister of Culture and Education, Minister of Tourism and, more challengingly, the College Principals.

The Olympic Flame for the Sydney Games, by coincidence, happened to be on tour of the island so there was great excitement. At the Olympic Reception, later that day, I was presented to the Prime Minister, Dr Terepai Maoate, who was very enthusiastic.

Thanks to The Commonwealth, when visiting places like the Cooks in the middle of the South Pacific and thousands of miles from the nearest habitation, one is made to feel immediately 'at home'. The people are charming and polite, they speak beautiful 'Queen's English' and are very well educated probably better than in the UK in many ways. They are also deeply religious with churches of every description around the island from Catholic, Church of Scotland, Church of England, Methodist to Seventh

Day Adventist and much more, and everything is, as expected, closed on Sunday.

To my surprise, I was invited this time to a St Andrews Society dinner – descendants from the missionaries as expected. I arrived and found twelve families of Scottish descent who appeared thrilled to see a genuine Scot. There were also some Cook Island VIPs present including a former Prime Minister, Sir Geoffrey Henry, and a former Queen's Representative, Sir Apenera Short.

They proceeded to go around the room telling me proudly about their Scottish heritage over several generations since 1820 when women were allowed to get married at age fifteen – they then asked me to respond.

En route home, I visited Trinidad & Tobago to see the Steel Band again to confirm their attendance at the 2000 show representing the West Indies. They had indicated that they would attend but they could not fund flights to Edinburgh, which was not surprising as the cost then was around £25,000.

In those days, The Tattoo expected overseas acts to fund their flights to Edinburgh – nor were they paid a fee – so you could say it was a big ask. This was a problem that we faced with many acts.

Despite various meetings in Port of Spain, I could not get them to agree and I could not get to see the Minister of Defence, so, exasperated, I flew home.

After I returned to the office, not giving up, I asked to see our sponsor, a well-known bank. My contact in the bank, who I knew well, agreed to have a lunch meeting. At our Tattoo Italian restaurant, *Rusticana*, on Cockburn Street, we had an excellent lunch and after some white wine with the first course and knowing my friend liked red wine, I ordered a good bottle of Barolo. Towards the end of lunch, he asked if all was well with the show.

I said, 'All was well but I have a small problem with my Steel Band from Trinidad. You see they can't afford the flights.'

'How much...precisely?' he asked.

To which I replied, '£20,000.'

'We'll do that,' he said. Problem solved.

I believe that some of the very best deals are made over a good lunch.

The *Rusticana* or *'Rustycan'* is it was known became The Tattoo restaurant where many deals were done and plans made. I had my own table which, by chance, had a map of the world on the wall behind me which became my planning map for overseas travels.

During The Tattoo in August, every day I would entertain a few Directors of Music, Pipe Majors and cast members. One day, we had the South Africa Navy Band and their talented, competent, young solo singer joined us for lunch, during which I asked what her favourite song was. I then asked her to sing it to the whole restaurant which was a memorable moment for us all – afternoon cabaret.

In June, I was invited back to Washington for 'The Spirit of America' show and stayed at the *Willard* as usual. I was determined to improve our relationship with the US authorities to acquire these excellent US Bands and acts more easily – if this was ever possible. This time, I was very well hosted by Colonel Gary Lamb and Lieutenant Colonel Tony Cason, the two very accomplished Directors of Music from Pershing's Own Band. I enjoyed the show and I met all the top brass. The following day, I had arranged to see a senior civil servant who worked in the Pentagon on all matters ceremonial. He advised me frankly that formal approval for US Army Bands and assets for The Tattoo was unlikely – they would be too long away, too expensive and it was not an approved way of employing US assets. US assets, I was told were for the people in the USA and this appeared to be the rather parochial Pentagon line, and strange, as the generals were all so keen.

I found out later that following my persistent requests, the civil servants had rewritten the rules to that effect just to make it difficult.

That evening, I was invited to the US Marines as I had asked to see their 'Beating Retreat'. Maybe it would be easier to persuade the US Marine Bands to come to The Tattoo? I witnessed a great 'Beating Retreat' ceremony in their ancient barracks built in 1801 with their top Washington Bands:

US Marine Band 'The President's Own', brass and woodwind.
The Bugle and Drum Corps 'The Commandant's Own', all brass and top class Drum Corps.
The Silent Drill Platoon Tossing rifles.
Two Companies with Colors On parade.

This was, without doubt, a stunning display of the highest order. I was impressed. It was all so professional and executed with great precision and expertise.

After the show, I was asked to the Officers' Mess for a drink. Sadly, the Commandant of the Marine Corps, General James Jones (who became National Security Adviser to President Obama), was away on duty. Thankfully, I still met all the key players and later asked the question:

'How can I persuade your wonderful bands to take part in The Tattoo?'

The senior Marine said to me, 'If the General says go – we go!'

That seemed more sensible than the Army attitude so I hoisted that in and realised I must meet this General.

On returning to Edinburgh, I was delighted to hear from Susan Lawton, our brilliant Box Office Manager, that for the first time in 50 years, we were sold out, and before First Night. Clearly, someone enjoys our show. Susan Lawton so deserved an accolade: she served The Tattoo for 30 years running our own box office with a small expert team.

The second big event of the year was a great honour for The Tattoo team: to produce Scotland's special musical tribute to HM The Queen Mother on her 100th Birthday on 27 July 2000.

A very special cast had been assembled and it was a rare moment to see a full house of Scottish Military Bands:

All the Scottish Military Bands Five (reduced due to MOD cuts).
All the Scottish Military Pipes and Drums Ten including the Gurkhas.
The Commonwealth Pipes and Drums Eight.
Highland Dancers and Pipes and Drums from Queen Victoria School, Dunblane
Guard of Honour from The Queen Mother's Regiment, The Black Watch

It was wonderful that a record number of excellent Commonwealth Pipes and Drums made a special trip for this event. They were determined to attend due to their admiration for HM The Queen Mother; they then stayed on for The Tattoo:

Black Watch of Canada The Queen Mother, then Colonel-in-Chief.
Cameron Highlanders of Ottawa
Toronto Scottish The Queen Mother, then Colonel-in-Chief.
Royal Victoria Regiment From Australia.
Cape Town Highlanders The Queen Mother, then Colonel-in-Chief.

Argyll and Sutherland Highlanders Of Canada.
Calgary Highlanders
Wellington and West Coast and Taranaki Regiments

I remember speaking to many of those Pipe Majors and Drum Majors who told me, as they did the BBC, that this was their finest hour – to march through the Drawbridge of Edinburgh Castle on such a prestigious occasion. For many of those great Commonwealth Bands, it was a 'once in a lifetime' opportunity. For us, it was an occasion that will never be repeated: All our fine Military Pipes and Drums and Bands and eight of the best Pipes and Drums from The Commonwealth.

The evening, which was attended by members of the Royal Family including The Duke of Kent and Princess Alexandra, went very well and we hoped that the massive sound would be heard in London by The Queen Mother. We played two of her favourite tunes, 'The Sound of The Pipes' composed for her by Wing Commander Barry Hingley RAF and 'Oft in the Stilly Night', which some years later was performed by the Massed Pipes and Drums at her funeral procession. It was unique and so memorable.

It was fitting on the Golden Anniversary of The Royal Edinburgh Military Tattoo that we should feature all the Scottish Pipes and Drums as they are and always will be the main pillar of The Tattoo. It was the biggest ever Massed Pipes and Drums to set foot on the esplanade of the Castle with fifteen bands and a record seven from The Commonwealth, as well as amazing Military Bands from the Royal Marines, Scots Guards and the Highland and Lowland Band of the Scottish Division; and from overseas, Maori, Mounties, Zulus, the Trinidad & Tobago Steel Band, and the South Australia Police Band. It was the biggest Edinburgh Tattoo ever, an inordinate celebration of the 50th!

This was a watershed moment, for in 2006, the Ministry of Defence formed The Royal Regiment of Scotland with the demise of all those wonderful Scottish Infantry Regiments. This was the last time their Pipes and Drums performed together.

The best news in 2000 was that for the first time ever The Tattoo was completely 'sold out'; an outstanding achievement by The Tattoo team and in future years this generated an increasingly early demand for tickets.

CHAPTER 7
2001

IT WAS COMFORTING to know that ticket demand was on the rise. I used to visit the box office daily to check on tickets and say that if we were not selling faster than last year then we were doing something wrong.

So, after a busy but successful year, another show was looming. Luckily, we had done plenty of advanced planning and had a breathtaking cast booked for August. However, I had to visit some of the acts to check their performance and timing before they got to Edinburgh and find some new international talent for future shows which included The Queen's Golden Jubilee in 2002. Consequently, I scheduled a programme of international visits.

Firstly, I had to return to Moscow, not the best moment as it was mid-February, this time to meet the Cossacks. It was Tolstoy who said, 'Russian History was made by the Cossacks'; a good reason for meeting them, perhaps.

I visited the Russian Cossack State Song and Dance Ensemble in Moscow. This was arranged by my two friends, Vitaly Mironov and Dr Dmitry Fedosov, who, amongst many other activities, ran the Moscow Caledonian Club. So it was back to the wonderful *Hotel Baltschug Kempinski*.

The next morning, over coffee, I met the director of the Cossack Ensemble, Leonid Milovanov, and his daughter who was one of the main dancers. At this meeting, she was the interpreter as well. We got on like a house on fire. I found the Russian people charming and keen to meet with us from the West. It did not take long to find an agreement. They would come to The Tattoo that year, and they bravely agreed to travel by bus from Moscow to Edinburgh – a journey of some 2,000 miles. Later, when they arrived in Edinburgh, they had just made it to Redford Barracks when the old bus blew up in a cloud of smoke and steam – a large and expensive bill followed!

I discovered at the end of the meeting that, in Russia, no agreement is formalised without some ceremony – I was kindly asked to lunch and as I followed the Cossacks through the back streets of Moscow, I became slightly concerned as to where we were going. Then we descended into a dark cellar furnished with a bare table with an embroidered tablecloth. There was no sign of lunch at all, but there was vodka and small glasses. Over many bottles, we toasted the Cossacks, The Queen, Scotland, Tsar Nicholas. It was a long but enjoyable session, and we struck up a firm friendship. Fortunately, I had one quiet night before returning to London.

The Cossacks turned out to be one of the finest examples of cultural dancing, with great music from a Balalaika Band and the most stunning, fast-moving well-choreographed dancing in superb colourful costumes. The crowd loved them.

In March, I had some important visits to make and also broke new ground as my first stop was China. The Tattoo had many visits over the years from our friends in Hong Kong and their excellent Police Band and Pipes and Drums, but never China and not the People's Liberation Army. But as they say, 'music crosses all boundaries', and it must be right to find some form of relationship with this vast country.

After a long flight of some 24 hours, I was met by the Defence Attaché's assistant, Sergeant Marx, who swished me into the centre of Beijing – a mass of contemporary skyscrapers and so much traffic, not just cars but bicycles, carts and all sorts amidst intense freezing smog. I was staying at a modest hotel near the Embassy, the *Hotel Jianguo* (used by the embassy), and as I entered the lobby, a full orchestra played familiar classical music. What a wonderful and civilised welcome to this extraordinary country.

I arrived at 11.15 am and, after a pause to unpack, I was invited to lunch with the Defence Attaché, Brigadier Gordon Kerr, and his wife, Issy.

Gordon had originally joined the Gordon Highlanders but, after his first tour in Northern Ireland, was recruited by the Intelligence Corps, in which he had an exemplary career in very challenging times. Despite the long flight, I was feeling on top form, but heeded the Defence Attaché when he told me after lunch to get my head down to recover before jet lag cut in; and his words were wise.

The next day, I met with the ambassador, Sir Antony Galsworthy – eight years in post and a fascinating man. He supported the idea of bringing China to Edinburgh but warned of the reaction by the Free Tibet

Movement and others. And as it turned out, he was right. He said he would inform Mr Geoff Hoon, the Secretary of State for Defence.

Next, the Defence Attaché had arranged a formal meeting with the PLA, and we arrived at this very grim and grey old barracks. We were met by about ten officers, mainly full colonels from the PLA, who sternly faced us at a long table. On my side, I had the Defence Attaché who spoke Chinese and a PLA captain who acted as interpreter. The senior PLA colonel, who was not overfriendly, strangely opened the meeting by making sure that we understood that the rank of colonel in the PLA was the same as Brigadier in the British Army. There followed a serious and challenging meeting in which we achieved the aim; they agreed to send a PLA contingent to Edinburgh. We were then introduced to the PLA Band of 50 playing in concert mode. They were extremely competent. Afterwards, I thanked the Director of Music who had kindly invited us to lunch, mercifully without the ten PLA colonels.

The last thing we expected was a smart lunch. The Director of Music, however, escorted us to the very smart Communist State Hospitality Restaurant. As we entered along a rather grand entrance and corridor, formed up on each side like a guard of honour, were the female staff, in pretty costumes, who bowed in welcome.

On sitting down, the Director spoke and said, 'Welcome, Honoured Guest we look forward to coming to Edinburgh. This luncheon is a gift from me to Honoured Guest and not from my party commissars.' (Two were in attendance.)

I was impressed by his bravado.

There followed a most delicious lunch of twelve courses. There were many enjoyable and meaningful exchanges between the Director and me through the competent captain-interpreter.

The lunch concluded with toasts of Chinese vodka before the Director said, 'Finally, we have a special presentation for Honoured Guest.'

In walked a woman who produced a wonderful Chinese instrument called a Pipa (sometimes known as a Chinese Lute) and gave us a short, impressive recital and then kindly presented me with this unique instrument.

Sadly, I never saw that very kind and somewhat politically incorrect Director of Music again. I have always wondered what happened to him and why he never came to Edinburgh.

My next stop was Sydney – a thirteen-hour flight via Tokyo. The main reason for visiting was that, following our successful Tattoo in New Zealand, I received an invitation for The Tattoo to perform in Australia for the first time.

On arrival, I was invited to tea with Dr Leo Schofield at his stunning *Bronte House* by Bronte Beach in Sydney. Leo is what you would call in Scotland, 'a well kent face' and is a highly regarded member of New South Wales Society, a former Director of Melbourne and Sydney Art Festival, an art critic and even a revered restaurant critic. On future visits, I was treated to the finest restaurants in Sydney – we ate well! *Bronte House* is renowned for its garden and its rare and beautiful collection of Frangipani.

It was really his inspiration and influence that resulted in The Tattoo coming to Sydney, although, by then, there were many other interested parties and impresarios offering deals.

Our rule at that time was that we did not wish to be managed/promoted by one of the big impresarios as their aim would be merely to line their pockets. Wellington was organised and promoted by the New Zealand Arts Festival, a charity and good cause financially supported by The Tattoo. In Sydney, Leo arranged that it would be the acclaimed 'Sydney Cricket Ground Trust'. On return to Edinburgh, we planned to make a decision about this exciting invitation.

Next, it was back to Wellington as I needed to line up support for The Queen's Golden Jubilee in 2002. There, I had meetings with the hierarchy – the Chief of Defence and the Chief of the Army, the latter being a touch unenthusiastic. I requested that his excellent and unique Military Band join The Tattoo for the Golden Jubilee, but I was surprised by his response:

'Well, you can have the Band, but I'm not spending a farthing on this!'

Thus, I succeeded in getting an agreement for the New Zealand Army Band, now acknowledged as one of the top Tattoo acts, but we would have to cover flights.

I later met my new friend, Captain David Clearwater, Director of Music of the Band, who had designed their unique style, 'comedy on the march', which our audiences loved. We spent two hours discussing the act for 2002. It would be a joint act: 'The Bands from Down Under' including Tonga and Australia.

Then, we gathered at what became my normal meeting venue, the *Dockside Restaurant*, which delivered the largest fish and chips in the world accompanied by fine local wine – deals were not a problem. I met the Chairman of the New Zealand Pipes and Drums Association, Nigel Foster, the President of New Zealand Pipes and Drums and Highland Dancing and the Dancing Director, Shirley-Ann Thompson, whose entire family danced – three generations. They all became good friends and agreed to join us in Edinburgh – the City of Wellington Pipes and Drums and a dancing group of twenty, all funded.

I was delighted with this success. I then flew via Auckland to the Cook Islands and on to a first visit to Tonga.

Since my last visit, the organising team had a mass of questions for me about The Tattoo, the barracks accommodation and the weather. I jokingly said it rarely rained in Edinburgh during August and later much regretted that as it turned out to be the wettest year on record.

The group was named 'The Cook Island National Youth Dance Team' and consisted of 58 male and female dancers from the main colleges in Rarotonga. I attended various brilliant rehearsals, each preceded and concluded by a prayer. The act was coming together and funded by the Island and my sponsor, Norwich Union.

On my free day, Papatua, my guide, took me to Aitutaki, one of the fifteen islands that make up the Cooks, a 45-minute flight and the world's best-kept secret. It is probably the most beautiful lagoon in the world; 9.3 miles by 7.5 miles with long deserted white beaches, palm trees, glorious turquoise water with swarms of tropical coloured fish and no sharks – paradise indeed.

On my last day, they asked me to a traditional Polynesian lunch. In the old days of Captain Cook and before the missionaries, cannibalism was rife on all the Polynesian Islands. I could not help thinking about the image in books of that large cooking pot. In fact, there is no pot, the cooking procedure is called Umukai and involves digging a large hole in the ground, which they showed me and creating a fire which produces red hot rocks. These days, happily, legs of pork and lamb are dropped into the hole and covered with palm leaves for four hours or so – I was safe!

The Cook Islands are beautiful – unspoilt, with stunning weather and the most charming and polite people I ever met. The islands, so far, are not ruined by tourism.

To get to Tonga, which is not that far from the Cooks, I had to do a dogleg of 2,000 miles back to Auckland and then 1,800 miles over the Pacific again. I had been advised by our excellent Defence Adviser to see the Tonga Defence Force Band.

I arrived at the capital's Nuku'alofa Airport, where I was greeted at the bottom of the steps by Captain The Hon Ve'ehala, Director of Music for The Tonga Defence Force and a cousin of the King. He was my charming guide for the visit and became a good friend. He ushered me into the VIP lounge.

Later, I was accommodated in a strange hotel by the sea called *The Dateline*, which needed a serious facelift. My room was so small that I was unable to get my case through the door. I had to ask for the bridal suite.

The day after, I met the High Commissioner, Derek Griffiths, who kindly looked after me. Later, we visited the Chief of Defence. That afternoon, I was invited to a reception and a band display at the Tonga Naval Base. I was so pleased and surprised to find this very talented Military Brass Band on an island miles from anywhere in the middle of the South Pacific. A must for The Tattoo.

I later found out that music is treated as special on the island and has a long tradition. The late Queen Sälote had made it compulsory for all children to play instruments and sing at school. It certainly paid dividends.

There followed a typically generous Tongan reception with presentations of garlands, all filmed by Tonga TV. Later, the High Commissioner gave a small reception and dinner in his smart residence by the sea and kindly invited some very senior Tongan officers and officials. He asked me to say a word or two about The Tattoo. Unfortunately, I made one of those classic jet lag errors by saying:

'It's such a great pleasure to be on this wonderful island of Fiji.'

They looked at me strangely. They were historical enemies with Fiji, but I think they forgave me.

The day after, I was taken for an audience with HM King Taufa'ahau Tupou V1, the King of Tonga. I was escorted by the High Commissioner, Derek Griffiths, in his Land Rover Discovery. The audience was held at the Summer Palace by the sea, a large, impressive, turreted, wooden building behind some grand gates, but there was no drive so the Land Rover drove onto the large lawn and parked at the front of the palace.

We were met by the Private Secretary wearing a Sulu (like a sarong or kilt) and no shoes. He showed us to the dining room, bedecked with Victorian lace curtains. We then awaited the arrival of the King.

The King, then 82 years of age, the son of Queen Sälote, and much loved by the people, had been 32 stone, impressive even by Tongan standards. However, there had been a celebration on the island as he had recently lost ten stone.

After some time, he appeared. He was on two sticks and had two hearing aids. We both bowed our heads; he sat down, then there was silence. After some time, I thought I should break the ice:

'Your Majesty, what a great honour and pleasure to be on your Island...'

He sort of woke up and then laughed. We then had a very memorable and jovial time. I asked him for his agreement to his band coming to Edinburgh. He said, 'Of course.'

It was a very great honour to meet the King who was charming, clearly very intelligent and with a great sense of humour. A few years later, I was to meet his son, Prince George, who by that time had succeeded to the throne. Prince George had been educated in England at The Royal Military Academy Sandhurst and spent several years with the 10th Hussars.

By my next visit, the Foreign and Commonwealth Office (FCO) had withdrawn the High Commissioner permanently – a new FCO economy and, in my view, a great mistake. That time, I had an audience with the new King George and, to my surprise, it was in the old High Commissioner's house.

King George said, 'You may wonder why I am here. I had to buy it as I loved the house, and they left their cats behind.'

I spent a fascinating two hours chatting with him about his time in the 10th Hussars and his great friend, Lord Glenarthur, who lives in Scotland.

I had agreed to visit Washington on my way home and endured another extreme journey of 18 hours via Honolulu and Los Angeles, arriving after midnight. The plan was to meet with the US Marines to try and secure them for the Golden Jubilee.

The following day, I was joined by my friend, Lieutenant Colonel Richard Quicke, 13th/18th Hussars, who was based with the British Defence and Liaison Staff and acted as a talented guide.

My meeting went well: they were keen to make it happen but, as ever, the Pentagon had to agree.

I was leaving for London the next day but, by chance, the Defence Attaché at the British Embassy asked to speak to me. I rang him immediately. He informed me that there was a 'senior' senator who wanted to see me. This was Senator John Warner, the US Naval Secretary and Chairman of the US Armed Services Committee, a distinguished American widely known as the 'American Aristocrat'. He lived in a rather grand house and was passionate about hunting and shooting – many said he should have been born an Englishman. Furthermore, amongst his three wives, he had been married to Elizabeth Taylor. For his service in strengthening the American-British military alliance, he was given an honorary knighthood by HM The Queen.

I could not imagine why this important senator wanted to see me or how he had heard that I was in Washington. I took a cab to Capitol Hill, where it was not difficult to find his large office. I waited in the outer office for ten minutes before being ushered through to meet him. I found a tall, elegant and charming man of stature. He showed me around his office.

'Here are the medals of my daddy.' (He was a US Marine in the Second World War.)

'Here is a photo of my current racehorses. Here are my paintings of flowers, and here is my hero.' [A sculpture of Winston Churchill.] Please sit down.'

I then said, 'Senator, it is a great privilege to meet you and indeed to visit Capitol Hill, but what can I do for you?'

He replied, 'I just want to visit that show of yours in Scotland. My background is Scottish, and I would like to bring my whole family.'

I responded, 'That would be a great pleasure. No problem, I will arrange a programme for you.'

He then said, 'What can I do for you?'

'I would like the US Marines, please,' I answered.

As you can imagine, this was the start of a very productive association – the special relationship working at last.

So, he came in August *en famille*, fully-attired in kilt order and accompanied by a charming and good-looking woman. I had arranged a special evening for him: a VIP guided tour of the Castle followed by dinner with the Governor of Edinburgh Castle and then watching the Tattoo from the Royal Box. When we got to St Margaret's Chapel at the top of the Castle (used by Scottish royalty since 1130), he disappeared inside with his lady friend for a long time. I was looking at my watch as we had a show to produce and the generals' dinner party. They then emerged looking rather happy; we completed the tour and an enjoyable evening followed.

Some months later, he rang me to thank me and said, 'You may have wondered why I was so long in that Castle Chapel of yours. I am pleased to tell you that I got engaged to my third wife, Jeanne Vander Myde.'

The result of this extraordinary meeting and friendship was the excellent US Marines Bugle and Drum Corps, which attended the 2002 Golden Jubilee Tattoo in the presence of HM The Queen and a smaller Marine Band for the whole month of August, which was a real triumph. He helped me with other Tattoos when the Pentagon was again proving difficult. I later found out from a friend in the Pentagon that the civil servant who was in charge of ceremonies and the allocation of all US Bands, who I had met before, was so annoyed that I had defeated the system.

Sadly, John Warner died in 2021. He had reached the great age of 94.

It was said in various obituaries that, had it not been for his marriage to Elizabeth Taylor, he would have been President of the United States of America. A real gentleman who I was honoured indeed to meet.

In July, I paid my annual visit to Nova Scotia, our sister Tattoo, started by my good friend Colonel Ian Fraser, Canadian Black Watch, who I have mentioned in a previous chapter. This time, however, it was a great pleasure to meet Major Aubrey Jackman, MBE, then adviser to Nova Scotia and one of the greatest Tattoo producers of all time. After serving in the Second World War, he became responsible for shows around the world but will mainly be remembered for Tattoos at Aldershot, Bath, and particularly the Cardiff Searchlight Tattoo, as well as ABF Pageants and the Silver Jubilee extravaganza at Wembley Stadium, and if that was not enough, The Royal Oman Tattoo, which he inspired and produced. He and Ian were an inspiration to me and huge supporters during my time and put up with my Tattoo efforts.

As ever, the show in Halifax was excellent. They were full of pride and joy as they had been granted the title 'Royal' by Her Majesty The Queen, so now the show was called The Royal Nova Scotia Tattoo. It was great news. I said to myself I must do something about the title of my Tattoo.

After my return, I took up the challenge and submitted an application using the correct governmental procedure. Months later, I was informed by a junior Minister in Scotland that we (The Tattoo) were too young at 50 years, and we should wait until our 60th birthday. We eventually did receive the 'Royal Title' just as I was leaving in 2007. For us and The Tattoo team, it was a great accolade.

During the two-hour show in Halifax, there was one act that stood out from the rest that year – a small Drum Corps of six drummers at the back of the arena performing a stunning drumming routine that was well choreographed; they even threw their sticks. My Production Manager, Steve Walsh, and I asked to see the leader at the end-of-show reception. This would be my first introduction to Erik Julliard from this Swiss Drum Corps from Basel.

After chatting, I said, 'Would you like to perform at our Tattoo?'

Looking at my tartan trews, he said, 'Do you mean THE Tattoo?'

I said, 'Yes', and so we agreed to 2003. I informed them that they would have to get bigger. They promised to grow to about twenty. This meeting was an extraordinary moment in history as, firstly, it led to the birth of the renowned 'Top Secret Drum Corps', which became one of the very few top tattoo acts in the world and, then later, led to the launch of The Basel Tattoo in 2006.

CHAPTER 8
2002

THIS WAS THE SPECIAL YEAR, the Golden Jubilee of HM The Queen. I knew the Private Secretary, Lord Robert Fellowes, quite well and since I had become the producer in 1995, I had been sending videos of the show to him for Her Majesty, which I was told she watched at Balmoral when on holiday. In addition, I had consistently written letters to Robert every year asking, 'When was Her Majesty coming to see The Tattoo?', as she had only been once as Princess Elizabeth in 1951.

I wrote again at the end of 2001 and, finally, in early 2002, I was delighted to receive the good news that she would be attending The Tattoo in August following The Commonwealth Games at Manchester – so the pressure was on.

I had been planning over two years for this great Jubilee with a special cast and the theme would be Britain and The Commonwealth. The main players of which were:

The Massed Pipes and Drums From the UK and The Commonwealth. Nearly a full house from the Scottish Regiments and great bands from Australia, Canada, New Zealand and South Africa.
Military Bands from The Royal Marines, The Scots Guards and the Royal Air Force A full house.
A *Massed Highland Dancing display from The Commonwealth.*

And a very nice surprise was that the Regiment assigned my son, Harry, my ADC.

Conscious that this was probably going to be the most important year for The Tattoo so far, I still had to secure some acts and also plan for future years.

I made a special visit to Bermuda, a self-governing British Overseas Territory. Although many people think it is in the West Indies, it is 800 miles to the north and close to the USA, just 650 miles, so the population is a mix of British, American and African.

A visit in the Jubilee year seemed to be appropriate and I had heard that they had a great Military Band.

On arrival, I received a warm welcome. I met the Commanding Officer of the Bermuda Regiment, the Head of the Bank of Bermuda, Mr David Scholfield, our close friend, and the Prime Minister, the Hon Jennifer Smith. I then witnessed a performance by the Bermuda Band at Warwick Barracks and attended a dinner in the Officers' Mess.

I was generously accommodated at the wonderful house, *Tideaway*, belonging to our good friend, Christopher Sharples. His father, Sir Richard Sharples, was Governor of Bermuda and, in 1973, was assassinated along with his aide-de-camp and his dog – a tragic story of racial tension on the island, now resolved.

I had also heard of the Gombey Dancers, traditional cultural dancers representing the time of African slavery when they performed in masks and costumes to hide their identity. Now it is part of the rich tradition on the island and their costumes are colourful and unique.

I invited the Regimental Band and Corps of Drums of the Bermuda Regiment and the Gombey Dancers for 2003.

In late February, I set off on my annual world tour beginning with the first of many visits to Oman.

The Sultanate of Oman is a best-kept secret – it is a spectacular place to visit. The capital, Muscat, is situated on the coast of the Arabian Sea and the Gulf of Oman with rocky mountains behind. Beyond these lies a beautiful desert with extraordinary rock formations. Since the coup in 1970, Oman has been ruled by Sultan Qaboos who made spectacular developments to the city and area: new mosques, hotels and roads; housing in the main areas is restricted to white buildings of no more than three stories, unlike Dubai and Abu Dhabi. It is a most impressive city: the motorways have flowers in the centre and are edged with mown grass, hedges and shrubs.

The Oman Forces still have a large team of British advisers and staff. I was visiting to find a suitable Military Band or Pipes and Drums and there was plenty to choose from as there are Military Bands and Pipes and Drums with The Royal Guard, The Royal Cavalry, the Army, the Air Force, the Navy and even the Police. There is an amazing variety of talent including Pipe Bands on horses and camels, women's Pipe Bands,

Steel Bands, Drum Corps, orchestras and much more. This array of talent has been largely inspired by Brigadier Ramis Bin Juma'an, Director General Military Music, with the encouragement and full approval of HM The Sultan. The quantity and quality are now unmatched in the Middle East, a great achievement.

On this occasion, I wanted The Royal Guard or the Army, which are difficult to acquire. Consequently, I was offered The Royal Oman Army Pipes and Drums and the Military Band with a British Director of Music, Major Anthony Hodgetts, and my old friend, Pipe Major John Bruce, who was my Pipe Major (Royal Scots Dragoon Guards) when I was in command. This was a good team and I asked them to put an act together comprising a Military Band, Pipes and Drums and cultural dancers, and I would return to see it on another visit.

I was kindly helped by my friend, Major General Robin Searby, who held the appointment of Special British Liaison Officer to the Sultan – an exalted appointment indeed, and this fascinating and demanding job comes with a charming house on the coast with a full staff and various official cars and jeeps.

The next stop was a return to Delhi to secure something for the Jubilee Tattoo. I stayed in *The Imperial Hotel*. Along with the *Oberoi*, it is one of the very best hotels in India. *The Imperial* is an oasis of peace in central Delhi with a garden and pool. Inside, it is like an Officers' Mess with uniformed staff and wall-to-wall military pictures including 'Scotland Forever' the charge of The Greys at Waterloo by Lady Elizabeth Butler. I felt completely at home.

On arrival that evening, I met Sanjoy Roy, an entrepreneur of the Arts and Director of Teamwork Arts, which produces performing arts, visual arts and literature festivals across 40 cities worldwide. He is a good friend and has helped me hugely regarding cultural acts for The Tattoo. I had the honour of meeting his father, the late Admiral Roy. The Admiral served with the Royal Navy before partition and then the Indian Navy. He invited me to lunch at the elite *Gymkhana Club*. (The club has an eighteen-year waiting list.) On the way in, we passed the ballroom – looking a bit shabby. He said they had not used it since the party held for the last Viceroy's departure. We had a gin and tonic and a luncheon of tomato soup, Irish stew and trifle. You could not get more British than that. But what a charming man.

I aimed to find a mounted detachment and a cultural act for the Jubilee year. It was so important, in my view, that India was properly represented. Culture first. So, early morning I was off to the domestic airport to catch a flight to Imphal (Manipur in NE India, the scene of crucial Second World War battles) where I was to meet my guide, Mrs Geetha Rao, introduced to me by Sanjoy. She had agreed to show me some martial arts and dancing groups. Since the Second World War, Manipur has been seeking independence so there is considerable unrest there. It is a secure area needing a special pass. Imphal is chaos, poor and underdeveloped. I visited the war memorial, which is an oasis of peace, huge and manicured. It appeared to be the only clean and tidy place in Imphal.

Geetha introduced me to a variety of wonderful local cultural art forms in and around the city:

Naga Tribal Dance
Martial Arts
Drumming

Eventually, although I loved the Naga traditional dancing, I selected Dhol Cholom, a dynamic drumming act and Thang-ta, a scary martial arts act by women, all presented by the Manipur Dance Company.

It had been an all-day session. That night, because the only decent hotel, the *Imphal*, had been destroyed in riots, I was put up in extremely run-down accommodation, the home of large cockroaches and so, for me, very unusually, I went to bed fully dressed and with the light on as cockroaches only appear in the dark.

The following day, before leaving, I was taken to meet the Governor of Manipur, Ved Prakash Marwah and I was greeted at this heavily-defended 'Raj Bhavan Compound' surrounded by huge walls, by a very impressive and smart Police Guard of Honour wearing full dress and Pagri.

On returning to Delhi, however, after a long adventure I have to say I was pleased to be back in the luxury of *The Imperial*.

The ensuing morning, I visited the President's Bodyguard (The Household Cavalry of India). The Commander was Colonel Malhi who presented me with a fine bay charger and we went for a wonderful ride along Mountbatten Ridge (named in his memory) within the Presidential

Palace grounds inhabited by flocks of parrots and peacocks. On our return to the stables, I was given a stunning display of Tent Pegging. We in the British Cavalry thought we were good at it but this was the best I had ever witnessed – I wish I could have put them on the esplanade.

After breakfast, I was collected and given a tour of the barracks and the horses. We agreed that a mounted detachment would attend The Tattoo – all being well. I was then taken to lunch in the Officers' Mess, with wives present; nothing seemed to have changed since the days of the Raj, including the Royal paintings, Regimental silver and photographs of previous Commanders. I was so impressed by their tremendous hospitality and kindness.

Before leaving India, I was taken to see the magnificent city buildings designed by the renowned architect, Sir Edwin Lutyens. He thought 'big': the Raj Path, longer than Champs-Élysées, is 2 miles long; the massive War Memorial Arch India Gate; and the elegant Parliament buildings leading to the old Viceroy's Palace, now the Presidential Palace, known as Rashtrapati Bhavan which is said to have a bigger footprint than Versailles. The other gracious buildings house the parliament and associated ministries including the MOD.

On this occasion, I met the Ministers and team for Tourism and External Affairs.

After an excellent and fascinating visit, I was off to Korea.

This was my first visit to South Korea and I was delighted to be met by the Defence Attaché, Brigadier John King.

En route to my hotel he said, 'We have a busy programme and you will really enjoy Korea, however, there are two things that I should warn you about: First they all eat something called kimchi which is made from fermenting cabbage and everyone and everything smells of it. You may not like it. Second, you have been invited as an honoured guest from the British Army to a Korean Army Banquet tomorrow at Army HQ and although it is now illegal, you will be offered DOG and as a guest they will give you the more interesting parts of the animal.'

There was a pause as I thought of returning to the airport.

Then he said, 'Don't worry, I said you were too busy to attend the Banquet!'

The reason for this visit was that several years ago I had been sent by a

Tattoo fan a small photograph of a stunning-looking band in yellow and technicolour uniforms. Fascinated, I tracked it down with the help of the Defence Attaché; I hoped to meet and to see this extraordinary Military Band, unknown in the West – The Traditional Band of ROK (Republic of Korea).

The morning after, I met the Ambassador whose grand residence was built in 1882 and with his enthusiastic support, we set off for the Army HQ, two hours south of Seoul. I assumed this was just a recce but, seeing the reception committee, I judged in true Korean efficient form, that this was a formal military visit. Luckily, I had learnt on my travels always to be prepared in terms of dress and always arrive bearing gifts.

We arrived at the smart HQ complex to be met by Major General Park and Brigadier General Kim who was Adjutant General. To my surprise, they had already had full authorisation by the Korean MOD for the Band to travel at their expense to Edinburgh and as yet I had not even invited them!

We then visited the band, which has a thousand-year history. In all my travels, I have never seen anything to compare with this unique body of musicians and drummers: soldiers in peacock yellow robes and broad yellow hats; others in red, white and blue costumes. What a kaleidoscope of colour.

The sound, however, was different and very Korean. It was, without doubt, most impressive and a must for The Tattoo.

A long meeting followed, and we were offered a traditional Korean tea which I am told is made from boiling water and an infusion of leaves, roots, flowers, fruits, grains, mushrooms and often seaweed. I have to say this was not one of my favourite beverages.

The next day was free so the Defence Attaché took me to see the war memorial to the Gloucester Regiment (The Glorious Glosters) at the Imjin River. We heard the story and viewed the battlefield positions. We also visited the DMZ (Demilitarised Zone) where we were given a fascinating briefing by the US Army which, still to this day, man the rather scary border and the checkpoint between North (the DPRK) and South Korea. It reminded me of the horrific border between East and West Germany in Berlin during the Cold War.

Next was the first of many visits to Hong Kong where our great friend,

David Scholfield, was Head of the Bermuda Bank – a quick stopover en route to Australia.

I was met at the airport and whisked by a smart Bermuda Bank car and driver, Erik, to the Scholfields who lived in a wonderful house on 'The Peak', 1,000 ft above the city.

In a day, I was given a fascinating tour of the old colony including Stanley Market and the excellent Hong Kong Club with a delicious lunch preceded by dry martini.

Then I was off to Australia for my second visit to Canberra. This time, I had to find agreement from the hierarchy to bring The Tattoo to Sydney. My first port of call was the High Commission to meet the Defence Attaché, Commodore Graham Wiltshire. We had a long and detailed discussion. First, I had to get the green light of approval from the High Commissioner, Sir Alastair Goodlad. Then I presented my case to the Chief of Defence Staff Australia, General P J Cosgrove, to request the support of the Australian Forces.

Sir Alastair agreed to the venture, indeed he was full of enthusiasm and offered to brief the Minister for Defence, Geoff Hoon, as we needed to get MOD approval for such a major event overseas involving around 1,000 troops. With stage one achieved, I was invited to a delicious lunch at the impressive High Commissioner's Residence and met his charming wife, Cecilia. Also present was Leo Schofield, the inspiration and the promoter from Sydney and the Defence Attaché – just the four of us. The High Commissioner agreed to speak to the Prime Minister, John Howard, and the Chief of Defence Staff. I could not have asked for more. Before leaving the residence, I slipped unnoticed behind the green and beige door to thank the staff and met a charming ex-Royal Marine chef and as I was chatting I was discovered by the High Commissioner. He said, 'Thank you so much, no one ever thanks my staff.'

One of the main acts for the Golden Jubilee was 'The Bands from Down Under', consisting of Australia, New Zealand and Tonga, so I had to visit all three acts to check the music and choreography. Each would be allowed just two or three minutes for their performance and then they would play together.

First, I went for the day to visit the Australian Military Band in Adelaide (10/27 South Australia Regiment). They are a reserve Regimental

Band and perfect for the job, clothed in old, scarlet uniforms with white helmets. I witnessed a performance with their Commanding Officer – all good well-known Australian music.

Content with them, I set off for Tonga via Auckland. As I boarded the rather small aeroplane, I noticed some disarray and a flurry of smart Tongans in Sulus. In the chaos, I took my place in the front right seat in business class. Outside the window, to my horror, I saw my large, bright blue suitcase being offloaded and replaced by a mass of boxes and new TVs. I knew that if I lost my case now, with the pace of my travel, I would never see it again so, I urgently asked the air hostess to rescue it.

She said, 'Please sit down, this may be difficult as the King [of Tonga] is about to board.'

Sure enough, at that moment, the 22-stone King appeared. As he took his seat (left front), I bowed deeply and I think he recognised me from my previous visit. We briefly chatted – my second audience with the King!

Then, as if that was not enough, a body was loaded accompanied by a funeral party. This was not the best day to travel. Then the good news, with great relief my case reappeared and was loaded, and with a very full and heavy aeroplane, a mass of shopping and boxes with the King and his entourage, we only just took off.

On arrival at the capital of Tonga, we were greeted by a huge Guard of Honour. I was met by the charming Major (recently promoted), Lord Ve'ehala, a cousin of the King, the Senior Director of Music. I was whisked through the VIP lounge behind the King.

The following day, which was extremely humid and 95 degrees Fahrenheit, I was invited to a full-scale VIP parade to witness the band performance of twenty minutes which was excellent. It was attended by the great and the good including High Commissioners of Britain and India and various Tongan VIP officials. There was an exchange of presents then the food was blessed and we enjoyed, as is traditional in Tonga, a massive lunch.

Subsequently, I flew to Wellington for the day, to persuade the New Zealand MOD to agree to release the Army Band and the excellent Director of Music, Major David Clearwater, who was about to be posted to East Timor. As usual, I was unsuccessful in finding an agreement for funding for travel but we would find a way. I then had a meeting with

David Clearwater who, as he was in the lead, had to put the 'Bands from Down Under' act together – a long planning meeting followed in the favourite Dockside restaurant and we had the act sorted. With little recent sleep, I was invited to attend The City of Wellington Pipes and Drums party which required some extra stamina.

Early the next morning, I left for Washington – a long haul of eleven hours to LA and then five hours to Washington but I did at least catch up on sleep.

Thanks to my meeting with Senator John Warner at Capitol Hill in 2001 and his generous offer of support, I received a most favourable response to my invitation to the US Marines for the Golden Jubilee Tattoo and I was invited to attend a meeting with the US Marines Staff in the Pentagon to tie up the details.

The agreement with them was:

Albany Band US Marines A very talented band in blue uniforms – 50 for the whole Tattoo. Including rehearsals and travel – four weeks.
Battle Color Detachment From Washington for The Queen's Night especially, consisting of:
Commandant's Own Dressed in red and white uniforms.
Silent Drill Platoon
Color Guard

The Battle Color Detachment rarely leaves the USA so this was a real tribute to the Golden Jubilee by the US Marines.

I was thrilled with this result now fully agreed by General James Jones, Commandant of the US Marines, who later became Armed Services Adviser to President Obama. I remember meeting him at Edinburgh Airport and his arrival in great style: the Commandant's own personal US Marine jet with the Commandant up front in his suite of rooms and at the back 110 US Marines. The General later attended The Tattoo in the Royal Box and we sat him behind The Queen and Prince Philip to whom he was presented.

I then left for home.

As mentioned, we had an impressive line-up for Her Majesty's Golden Jubilee.

The highlights were:

Thirteen Pipes and Drums For the last time the Pipes and Drums of all Scottish Regiments were present (before defence cuts) and top bands from The Commonwealth: Australia, Canada, New Zealand and South Africa.
Tri-Service Bands A rare moment with Royal Marines, Scots Guards and Royal Air Force performing together.
Massed Commonwealth Highland Dancers From Australia, Canada, New Zealand, South Africa and home.
The 'Bands from Down Under'
Diol Cholom and Thang Ta The cultural group from India.
Trumpetterkorps Bereden Wapens Representing Europe, they entranced audiences with their First World War Bicycle Band playing 'Tulips from Amsterdam', which I was told was one of The Queen's favourites.
US Marines Probably the best Marching Brass Band in the world.
Royal Scots Dragoon Guards Action display.

In the finale, we presented the Scottish State Coach escorted by mounted detachments from The Household Cavalry, Royal Scots Dragoon Guards, The Royal Canadian Mounties, Lord Strathcona's Horse and the 61st Cavalry from India.

Her Majesty The Queen was greeted by a Royal Guard of Honour from the Highlanders, a detachment from The Royal Company of Archers, the General Officer Commanding Scotland, Major General Robert Gordon, and the Board of Directors. I was in the production box nervously smoking my Davidoff cigar with my excellent team waiting to cue the Jubilee fanfare at the split-second moment with the flypast by the Red Arrows. Luckily, it was a perfect start.

The show went very well thankfully, everyone in the 1,000-strong cast gave their best. At the end of the finale, I formed up the production team behind the Royal Box and as The Queen appeared, I was presented by Major General Gordon.

I said, 'Your Majesty, your presence tonight is such a great honour for The Tattoo.'

CHAPTER 8 - 2002

Her Majesty smiled and said, 'Well, you have been writing to me for the last seven years!'

I was amazed that she had seen all my letters to the Private Secretary.

Before the departure of The Queen, we organised for Her Majesty and Prince Philip two lines on the esplanade of the main players, the Directors of Music, Pipe Majors, Drum Majors and Heads of Cast – so they met them all. I presented the A-Team line. Every Pipe Major and Director of Music as well as heads of all the acts met Her Majesty.

Halfway along the line-up, I said, 'Ma'am may I present Pipe Major Amanda Smith, Pipe Major of The Tasmania Police, her father was a Pipe Major before her and started the band.'

There was a pause.

Her Majesty turned to me and said, 'I am sure it was her grandfather who started that band. Amanda responded, 'You're absolutely right, Ma'am, my father was a piss poor player.'

Her Majesty grinned. How on earth had she remembered?

Her Majesty left just before midnight after a most memorable evening for us all and The Tattoo – its finest hour.

We later received a nice letter from Buckingham Palace and the Private Secretary:

Dear Mel
The Queen and The Duke of Edinburgh have asked me to thank you for all that you did to ensure last night's Military Tattoo was such a huge success. As I am sure was evident both Her Majesty and His Royal Highness much enjoyed the performance and I know that The Queen was very touched by the tributes paid to her to mark her Jubilee. It was the best possible final event in the long Jubilee summer and Her Majesty was particularly keen for me to pass on her gratitude to you for masterminding such a marvellous spectacle.
Yours ever
Robin Janvrin
Private Secretary to The Queen

PICTURE GALLERY

BUCKINGHAM PALACE

The Royal Edinburgh Military Tattoo is in now in its 74th year and goes from strength to strength entertaining 230,000 people on the esplanade of Edinburgh Castle each year and an estimated worldwide audience of 100 million through BBC World.

The cast of around 800 is mostly made up of our excellent Pipes and Drums, Military Bands and Acts from home and since its inception it has also been hugely supported by The Commonwealth and performers from around the world.

As a spectator it is not entirely obvious how much work and planning goes on behind the scenes to make the show so very special. This book tells the story of the extensive travels of one particular Tattoo Producer, his meetings with various leaders and heads of state. Together with some amusing moments, it demonstrates the skill of negotiation and diplomacy required to entice the very best performers to travel across the world to Edinburgh and give their services free of charge for four weeks in August. It also highlights some of the historic moments for the Tattoo including the visit by Her Majesty The Queen in 2002.

The Royal Edinburgh Military Tattoo, with its magnificent backdrop of Edinburgh Castle, maintains its reputation as the world's premier Tattoo. It is also an essential flagship for Scottish tourism as well as contributing annually around £1million to Service Charities and the Arts. All of this, in no small part, thanks to the author of this book, Mel Jameson.

Anne

HER ROYAL HIGHNESS THE PRINCESS ROYAL

Lieutenant Colonel Richard Hambleton, Financial Director and
Steve Walsh, Production Manager (1995)

Cast Lunch at Easter Logie (1995)

Gazelle Helicopter Transporting Some of the 1995 Cast
to Easter Logie for Lunch (1995)

The Pipes and Drums of the Egyptian Army (1995)

The Gate to the Khyber Pass (1996)

New Zealand Police Pipes and Drums Competing at Invercargill (1996)

Pipe Sergeant in the 8th Kashmir Regiment Pakistan (1996)

US Army Silent Drill Display Team (1996)

Highland Dancer (1997)

Fiji Warriors in Fiji (1997)

Fiji Army Band and Warriors (1997)

Drum Major of the Fiji Army Band (1998)

REPUBLIC OF FIJI MILITARY FORCES
OFFICERS MESS
COMMANDERS LUNCHEON ON THE OCCASION OF
THE VISIT OF BRIGADIER M.S.JAMESON CBE.
TUESDAY 24 MARCH 1998

MENU

ENTREE
FRESH WALU KOKODA FROM THE BLUE LAGOON
COATED WITH COCONIT CREAM

SOUP
AVOCADO SOUP

MAIN COURSE
ROAST LEG OF PORK
COATED WITH BROWN SAUCE AND APPLE SAUCE
SERVED WITH CAESAR SALAD
DALO AND FRENCH FRIES

DESSERT
FRESH FRUIT SALAD FROM TAVEUNI
SERVED WITH ICE CREAM
TOPPED WITH STRAWBERRY SAUCE

TEA AND COFFEE
CHEESE AND BISCUITS

Menu for Lunch with Commander of the Fiji Defence Forces (1998)

Cook Islands Dancers (1998)

Barbados Army Band (1999)

Zulus From the Zulu Battalion (Mtubatuba Kwa Zulu), Natal (2000)

Adelaide Mounted Police (2000)

The Tattoo Performs in New Zealand –
Massed Pipes and Drums (2000)

The Tattoo Performs in New Zealand – The Finale (2000)

Bermuda Gombey Dancers (2001)

The Bermuda Regiment Band (2001)

Cook Islands Dancers (2001)

Cossack Dancer (2001)

The Queen Meets the Cast of The Queen's Golden Jubilee
Edinburgh Military Tattoo (2002)

The Queen's Golden Jubilee Edinburgh Military Tattoo
[Painted by Douglas N Anderson] (2002)

Visit by The Queen to The Golden Jubilee
Edinburgh Military Tattoo (2002)

Ramillies The Drum Horse of The Royal Scots Dragoon Guards
and a Mounted Troop of The Life Guards (2002)

Mounted Troop From The Royal Scots Dragoon Guards with
Ramillies the Drum Horse (2002)

The New Zealand Army Band (2002)

Police Guard of Honour at the Visit to the
Governor of Manipur (2002)

Traditional Army Band of Korea (2003)

Royal Palace in Tonga (2003)

Visit to 61st Cavalry, Jaipur, India (2003)

Traditional Army Band of Korea Dancers (2003)

Traditional Army Band of Korea Dancers (2003)

Gombey Dancers From Bermuda (2003)

Traditional Dancers From the Royal Palace, Oman (2003)

The Princess Royal, Melville Jameson and
the Lord Provost, Lesley Hinds (2003)

US Army Silent Drill Display Team (2003)

Top Secret Drum Corps (2003)

Top Secret Drum Corps (2003)

HRH The Princess Royal Talks to the Cast After The Tattoo (2003)

The Massed Pipes and Drums March on From The Drawbridge (2004)

Cheraw Dancers From India (2004)

The People's Liberation Army Display Team From China (2004)

The People's Liberation Army Band China (2004)

Club Piruett Gymnastic Team From Estonia (2004)

The Band of the South African Navy –
Director of Music, Commander Mike Oldham Plays the Solo (2004)

The Royal Air Force Massed Bands Drum Major (2004)

Highland Dancers (2004)

Rowena Macrae – Solo Violinist at the Finale (2004)

The Massed Bands of The Royal Marines Celebrate
The 200th Anniversary of the Battle of Trafalgar (2005)

The King's Guard of Norway (2005)

The Imps Motorcycle Display Team (2005)

The Finale (2005)

Trinidad and Tobago Steel Orchestra (2005)

Khattak Dancers From the Khyber Regiment Pakistan (2005)

The Finale of The Edinburgh Military Tattoo,
Aussie Stadium, Sydney (2005)

The Massed Pipes and Drums Emerge From the Drawbridge (2005)

Kung Fu Display From China (2006)

Prince Edward, Earl of Wessex (2006)

Watoto Orphans Choir, Uganda (2006)

New Zealand Army Band (2006)

Army of Chile Concert Band With Melville Jameson (2006)

Argentinian Patricios Regimental Band (2006)

The Finale (2006)

The Royal Edinburgh Tattoo (2006)

Sean Connery Presenting Edinburgh Castle to Melville Jameson
at his Farewell, Mel's ADC, Captain Richard McClure, on Right (2006)

The Massed Bands of The Coldstream and The Scots Guards
Joined by the Army Band From Chile (2006)

The Three Tattoo Producers:
Melville Jameson (Royal Edinburgh Military Tattoo),
Erik Julliard (Basel Tattoo) and
Brigadier Alfrey (Royal Edinburgh Military Tattoo) (2007)

Canadian Mounties at Windsor (2007)

Royal Arrival by Carriage, Windsor (2007)

Tank Commander Melville Jameson (2007)

HRH The Princess Royal, Tattoo Rehearsals, Redford Barracks (2007)

Massed Pipes and Drums Rehearsing Outside
St Basil's Cathedral, Moscow, for the Kremlin Zoria Tattoo (2007)

Fireworks Over Red Square at the Finale of the
Kremlin Ziora Tattoo (2007)

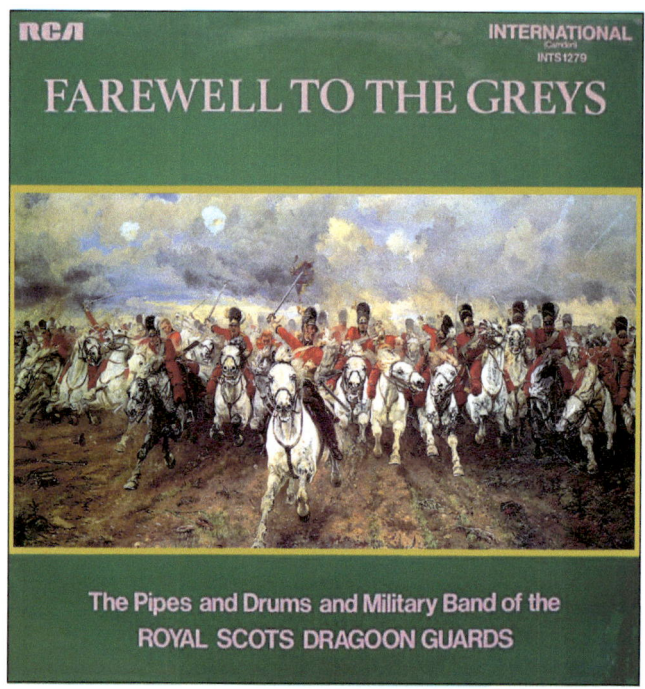

'Farewell to the Greys', The Pipes and Drums and Military Band of The Royal Scots Dragoon Guards (1972/1995) LP Record

7" Single of 'Amazing Grace'

The Edinburgh Military Tattoo Programme, 2001

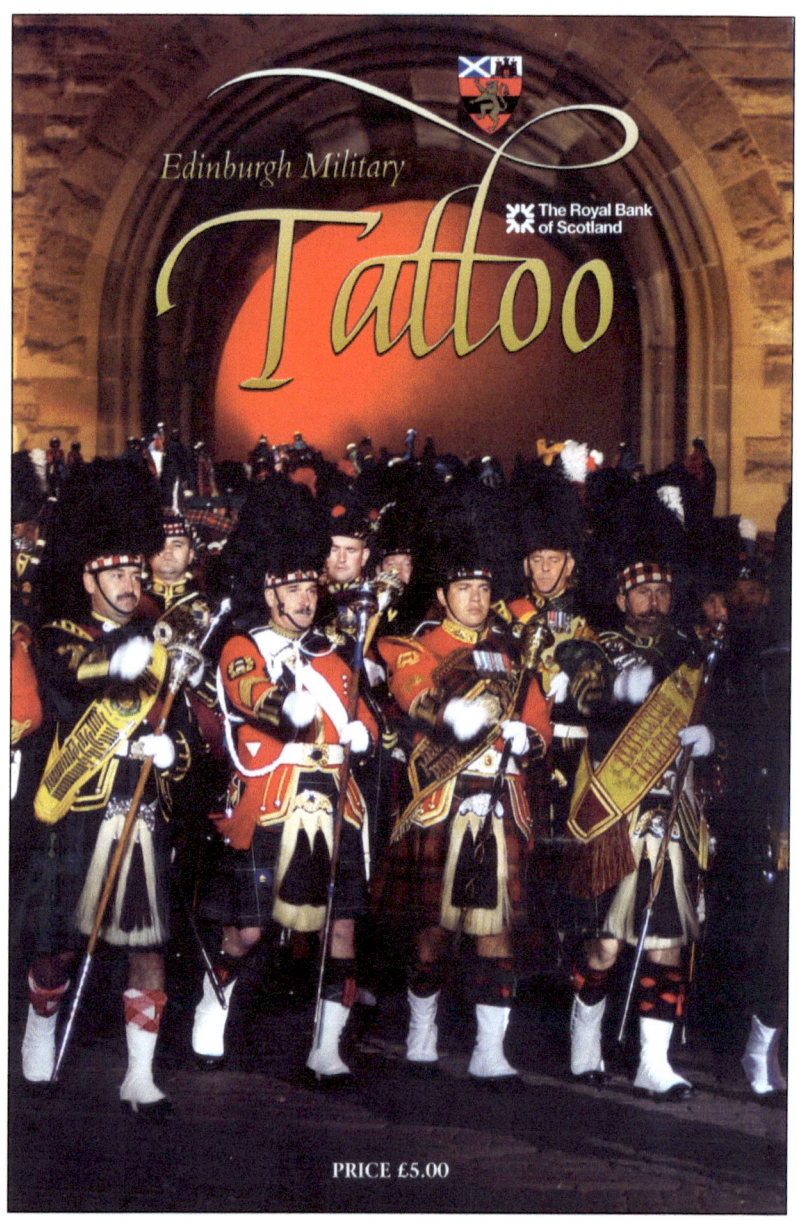

The Edinburgh Military Tattoo Programme, 2003

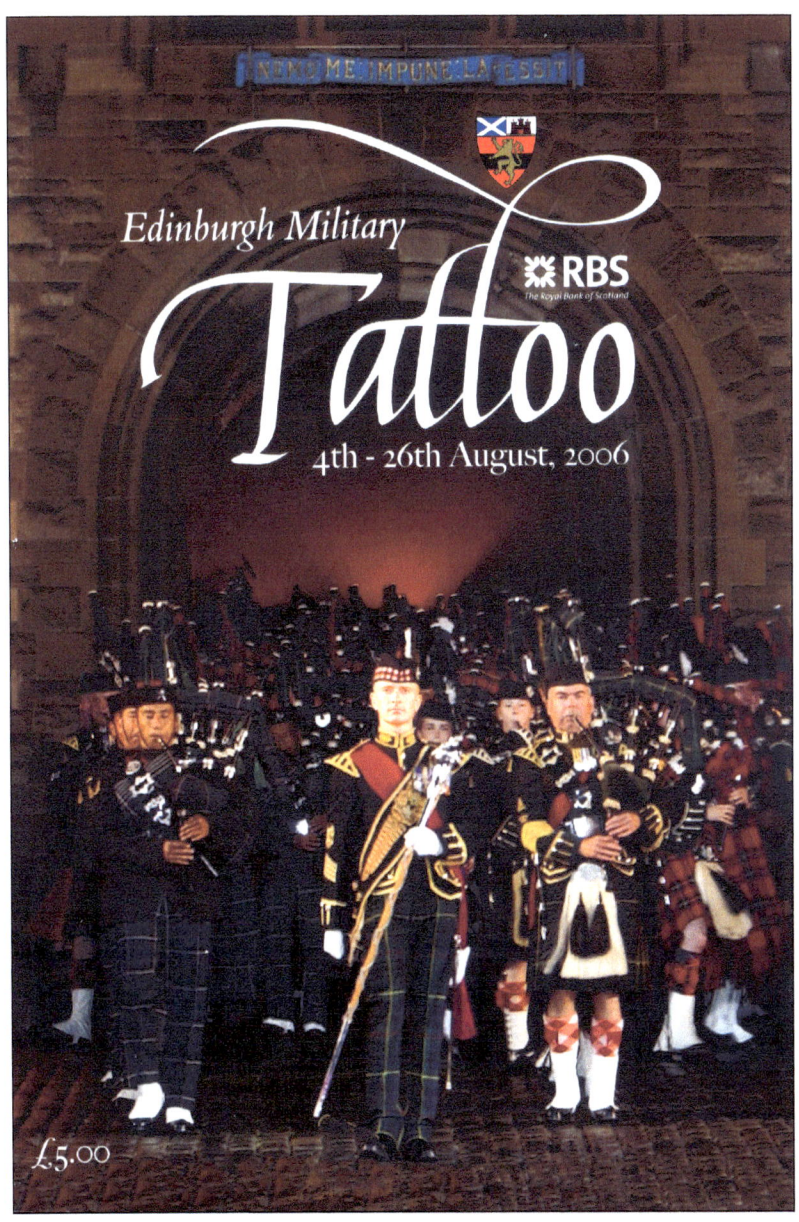

The Edinburgh Military Tattoo Programme, 2006

Brigadier Sir Melville Jameson

CHAPTER 9
2003

ACCORDINGLY, with the Golden Jubilee behind us, 'the show must go on'. We had a great line-up for 2003 after all my travels, some brand new acts and, indeed, some surprises. But we sadly said goodbye to the Director of The Massed Pipes and Drums, Major Gavin Stoddart, BEM, MBE, on his retirement. His contribution to the success of The Tattoo was immense. Nonetheless, we warmly welcomed his successor, Captain Stuart Samson, MBE, a Gordon Highlander, highly regarded in the Army and well-known across Scotland for his expertise with the Highland bagpipes. He became invaluable, a past master with the Massed Pipes and Drums, their playing and formations. After The Edinburgh Tattoo, in retirement from the Army, he became the supremo for The Basel Tattoo Massed Pipes and Drums and an esteemed piping judge in Scotland.

It was again time to go travelling, starting with India, to which I had been invited back.

The previous year, I had booked the President's Bodyguard for the Golden Jubilee. They had warmly accepted the invitation to provide a detachment to ride with the escort to the Scottish State Coach. At the very last minute – three weeks before rehearsals – I was informed that due to operational commitments, they were unable to attend which was really sad and alarming given the short notice. However, during the rehearsals, I was telephoned by the 61st Cavalry, the second ceremonial mounted regiment in India. They said, 'Would you like us to take the place of the President's Body Guard?' I was thrilled and agreed that we would provide horses and everything; they just needed to get here and they did, within two days! They performed brilliantly for the show; it was the start of a warm friendship and association with the 61st Cavalry.

I found that everyone I met in India was warm, friendly and extremely positive about their relationship with Britain, particularly in the Army and Navy, even at the highest level, where I found so much in common and a rare special relationship. They always wanted to help and join us in Edinburgh but sadly their enthusiasm was never matched by their politicians who were normally negative and unhelpful.

In India, I was accompanied by my wife, Sarah, which was a rare pleasure and a one-off. She would admit to not being a wildly enthusiastic traveller. Also, importantly, someone had to 'Keep the Home Fires Burning' given I was away so often.

We were being hosted by the 61st Cavalry and staying in the outstanding *Imperial Hotel* in Delhi. One of the officers, Major Rathore of the 61st, was our guide and invited us to the Republic Day Parade – my second visit. This time it was the dress-rehearsal. We had excellent seats so we could examine all the bands at close quarters.

The standard was extraordinary: 10,000 troops from the three Services, marching contingents each of a hundred with Military Bands and Pipes and Drums from the famous Indian Army Regiments such as the Dogra, Jat Guard and Mahar, Ghurkha, and from the Navy and Airforce, alongside a mass of military equipment and threatening rockets. There were cultural dancers from the Punjab, Mizoram, Bombay and more. Finally, the very charming camels of the Border Frontier Force and stunning Indian elephants. Wonderful!

The parade ended with the massive flypast.

It was undoubtedly the most magnificent spectacle of military precision, ceremonial style and panache. I suspect it is now the biggest and most colourful parade in the world.

The next day, we were driven to Jaipur, the Pink City, a journey of around four hours and we were booked into *The Rambagh Palace Hotel.* I had been invited for an official visit to the 61st Cavalry.

On arrival, we were taken to watch the polo at the Jaipur Polo Ground as a guest of Colonel Pinka Virk, Commandant of the Regiment. In the evening, we attended a reception and were honoured to meet the Maharana of Udaipur and the Maharani of Jaipur. The 61st Cavalry, amongst other ceremonial duties, are responsible for the polo at Jaipur and Delhi and organise the Indian National Polo Team.

In the morning, I was invited for an official visit to the 61st Cavalry based in Jaipur. The 61st was formed on partition in 1947. They are an amalgam of twelve mounted cavalry regiments of the Indian Army. I thought this would be an informal visit but quite the reverse, it was a full ceremonial event which was a great honour. The main items in the programme were:

> *Being welcomed by a mounted Guard of Honour carrying lances and a general salute.*
> *Meeting the Commandant, Colonel Pinka Virk, in his office.*
> *Being invited to inspect the horses (and present them with carrots but one of the horses did not like carrots and had to have an apple!).*
> *A tour of the barracks in the grand Regimental carriage.*
> *A formal luncheon in the Officers' Mess preceded by gin and tonic.*
> *Being presented with a stunning silver 61st Cavalry silver statuette.*

It was a memorable day and resulted in a formal Commonwealth affiliation between the 61st Cavalry and my regiment, The Royal Scots Dragoon Guards.

That evening, along with our friends, Bobby and Lulla Stewart, who were travelling with us, we were greatly honoured by an invitation to the amazing Red City Palace by HH Brigadier Bhawani Singh, MVC, Maharaja of Jaipur, known to his friends as 'Bubbles', for drinks and dinner.

The next day, we left for Delhi but we had not travelled far when our driver became very ill with what is well known as 'Delhi Belly' – not a nice experience. A disrupted journey of six hours followed.

Back in Delhi, it was all go, drinks and dinner with my friends, Admiral and Sanjoy Roy. I was introduced to the Indian Director of Culture, Vishwas Mehta, who invited us to witness an Indian cultural dancing audition especially laid on for The Tattoo. It was perfect, we could not do better than that.

The following day, I was first taken to meet the Adjutant General of the Indian Army at their Ministry of Defence in the wonderful Lutyens' buildings. We got on like a house on fire and when I asked for a Military Band and Pipes for the forthcoming year, he said that would be no problem and that we would have the most colourful and the best. The focus was Major Kacker who would keep me informed. I thought that was too easy.

And it turned out it was, as sadly a month before the show, Major Kacker sent me a military 'signal' saying in old-fashioned, polite speak:

'*Sir I have the honour to inform you that our Band and Pipes and Drums will now not be able to attend the Tattoo – I remain sir your humble and obedient servant.*'

So that was that and I can only surmise that again the Indian politicians had not given clearance to the Army. I then, at very short notice, had to fill an unexpected gap in the programme.

That evening, Sarah and I were collected by our new friend, Vishwas, and taken to the promised cultural display of dancing. We sat on two solitary chairs in a vast marquee. Then all the cultural groups performed for us – an audition indeed! The dancers came from most of the states in India – Punjab, Assam, Orrisa, Rajasthan, Gujarat and Mizoram. With difficulty, as there was so much talent, we selected Cheraw from Mizoram – a bamboo dance, unique and charming. Upon meeting the group afterwards, we found they were young, of college age, and spoke perfect English. I asked how this was and the leader told me that they come from a Catholic state and everyone speaks English. I booked them for 2004 and was informed that all expenses for travel would be covered.

We could not leave India without seeing the Taj Mahal at Agra but, after the last driving experience, we took the train to Agra – fast, punctual and clean. We were staying in the new *Oberoi Hotel* and they collected us in the typical Indian much-loved car, the Hindustan Ambassador, modelled in 1957 on the lines of the Morris Oxford and still very much in vogue and used as Staff Cars by the Army and Government hierarchy.

As we drove towards our hotel, I asked the driver – dressed in full Indian dress and Pagri – about the impressive house on the hill to our right.

He paused and said, 'Saab, the old British Governor lived there.'

I said, 'What a great place to live! What happened to him?'

He replied, 'He was killed in the Indian Mutiny.'

We arrived at the spectacular *Oberoi Hotel* in time for dinner. This hotel has to be the best we had ever experienced, superb in every way.

At dinner, I asked the head waiter, 'Is Mr Oberoi here today?', as I knew him well. (I met him in London and Delhi on my first visit.) We wanted to enthuse about his new hotel – minutes later his son, Vikram, whom we had not met came to our table and sat chatting for twenty minutes. He was charming like his father.

At dawn, from our bedroom window, we witnessed the spectacular sight of the Taj tinged with pink and yellow emerging through the morning mist, stunning and completely memorable.

We then had an early visit to the Taj Mahal before the crowds. It was truly magnificent.

On our route back to Delhi, we drove to the huge, red and impressive Agra Fort, known as the Red Fort, built in 1565 by the Mughal Emperor Akbar.

Not so nice were the dancing bears that we saw by the roadside, chained and with a rope through their nose, so cruel. I hear now that they are being rescued and taken to a bear park.

The other extraordinary and unmissable event held in Delhi during the Republic Day celebrations is the massive Beating Retreat which is in a different league to Britain's and probably the biggest in the world.

Major Gupta escorted us to this event amidst the chaos of traffic.

The backdrop is the Lutyens' Presidential Palace with camels dressed in amazing trappings and the Border Security Force standing perfectly still, silhouetted against the sunset, and each side of the square with the 61st Cavalry lining the flanks, an unbeatable and memorable set to the event.

The President of India arrived, escorted by the President's Bodyguard. Then fifteen Military Bands in spectacular uniforms marched onto the parade, followed by fifteen Pipes and Drums. It was an extravaganza of huge proportions, ceremonial colour and military music.

One of the highlights was the evening hymn which they play every year in memory of Mahatma Gandhi. It was his favourite, 'Abide with Me'. It was a fitting end to a fascinating and enjoyable visit.

After a pause at home, it was time to visit some of the acts abroad – a slightly shorter trip this year after India.

My second visit to Oman's Muscat was to check out the act from The Royal Oman Army for the 2003 Tattoo. This time I was invited to stay with General Robin Searby, the Senior British Loan Service Officer to HM Sultan Qaboos and his wife, Caroline, in their house on the sea at Haramel village, near Muscat. I was collected in a large, heavily air-conditioned Mercedes by Dawish, his driver.

It was the weekend (Friday), so I was invited for a drive into the spectacular mountain desert area where we had a picnic in true British Style: 'Mad dogs and Englishmen go out in the midday sun'. We joined up with the British Ambassador, Stuart Laing, and his wife, Sibella.

The next day, I was given a performance by The Royal Army Military Band, the Pipe Band and traditional dancers from the Palace of the Sultan, all nicely choreographed and rehearsed. We then discussed the strict regulations for a Moslem group with women – separate accommodation, and specific food with their chefs. And do we have a mosque in the Castle. No, but we would create one for them at Redford Barracks.

I was given a delicious Omani lunch by the Commander of The Royal Oman Army, General Ahmed Harith Al Nebhani, in the grand Officers' Mess. And finally, a drink in the Army Warrant Officers' and Sergeants' Mess with my friend, Pipe Major John Bruce, which in true Regimental form went on a bit.

En route to Australia, I had to revisit both South Korea, to check on the ROK Band Act for 2003, and China, to progress the act for 2004. It took three years and three visits to persuade the PLA China to come to Edinburgh, hugely helped by the excellent Defence Attaché, Colonel Gordon Kerr, and his delightful wife. I stopped briefly in Hong Kong for some R&R and a memorable lunch with David and Ballou Scholfield at the China Club.

In Sydney, I met up with my Number 2, Lieutenant Colonel Richard Hambleton, Financial Director of The Tattoo. We had some serious meetings in Sydney to prepare The Tattoo for performances in 2005. Richard carefully scrutinised the contract which we later agreed with the Sydney Cricket Ground Trust.

We had to select a stadium for the show so we visited various stadiums including the Sydney Cricket Ground, hallowed turf, which was too spread out, the Olympic Stadium, which was too vast (it held 115,000 for the Olympics and had been downsized to 82,000; it was too big and lacked any intimacy and would be a nightmare to 'light' effectively). Consequently, it was to be the Aussie (Rugby) Stadium, which with our Castle backdrop, would seat around 30,000.

We then flew to Canberra.

I was most impressed and relieved that the British High Commissioner, Sir Andrew Goodlad, was totally in support and seemed to have complete confidence that we could pull it off. The prospect of a tattoo in Sydney was a huge challenge for us and we still had to convince the three Services of Australia to join us.

In outline, we planned a 2-hour tattoo with a huge cast of 1,500:

Fourteen Pipes and Drums
Seven large Military Bands
200 Highland Dancers
Other acts from Australia and overseas

It was a mainly British and Australian cast.

A meeting followed at AUS MOD with the Staff of the Chief of the Defence Force: the Royal Australian Navy, Royal Australian Army and the Royal Australian Air Force. I gave them a full briefing on the proposed tattoo as we had to obtain the blessing of the Chief of Defence Force and his full support. Of course, for us, it was not just the show that had to be organised, it was a massive administrative and logistic military and civilian challenge to provide for the cast of 1,500. This included accommodation, feeding, air travel, transport as well as all the technical requirement for sound and light and an arena plan. As I had hoped, the Australian team were onside and very enthusiastic but we had to wait for a decision from the hierarchy.

In the afternoon, Richard and I were summoned to a meeting with the National Capital Authority for Canberra. Realising that we were producing a tattoo for Sydney, they wanted a tattoo as well! I explained the difficulties of moving such a large show with many people and acts. I did, however, offer the possibility of a smaller ceremony at the impressive War Memorial, the most important building in Australia.

We suggested (to be confirmed), a Tri-Service Beating Retreat on Australia Day, 26 January 2005. This plan went down well and the War Memorial Staff were delighted. (This is covered in a later chapter.)

Back in Sydney, I was overjoyed to meet an old friend from Perthshire, Christopher Dawson, who had just retired as Mayor.

Finally, before leaving, I met up with Leo Schofield for drinks at his home, *Bronte House*. Leo, the inspiration of The Edinburgh Military Tattoo performing in Sydney, had agreed to lead the promotion of

The Tattoo and would find a professional team to set it up. We discussed marketing, of course. He said Australia has watched The Edinburgh Tattoo on Television through BBC World every Christmas for 50 years along with The Queen's Speech, so there would not be a problem selling tickets. I then realised that we had better produce a show which met the expectations of all those 'Down Under'.

A return to Washington for some important meetings was the next stage of my journey. I revisited The Old Guard (3rd US Infantry Regiment) at Fort Myer. They are like The British Household Division, the Official Army Ceremonial Unit for the USA and Escort to the President, and they do it well.

I had requested the US Army Drill Team and had the backing of the Commanding Officer, Colonel Jim Laufenburg, and the 2-Star Commander.

That afternoon, I met with Senator John Warner (who I first met in 2002) at the US Senate. He gave me 30 minutes of his time on a busy day. Following my meeting, he was due to see President George W Bush and then appear on CNN.

It was the perfect opportunity to thank him for providing the US Marines to The Queen's Golden Jubilee and to ask for more help. He agreed to support the US Army Drill Team returning to Edinburgh. He asked for a visit to The Tattoo and this time would bring the Chief of the US Army, General Shinseki.

Before leaving the next day, I gave a lunch party for the key players at my favourite restaurant in Washington, the *Old Ebbitt Grill*, the oldest Saloon in Washington and the finest hamburgers.

On my way home, I decided to visit Bermuda to attend a rehearsal for the act by the Military Band and Gombey Dancers.

On arrival, I noticed an article in the local paper, *The Royal Gazette*, saying, 'Why on earth is The Edinburgh Tattoo inviting the Gombey Dancers to perform with our fine Bermuda Band?' I had caused a bit of a storm.

I thought it was essential to include this iconic folk group in the ceremony to represent Bermuda properly.

My first point of call was a meeting with the Governor, Sir John Vereker, in the vast Governor's residence, who appeared to be enthusiastic about my efforts so far. And, as Governor, he was de facto Commander in Chief of the Army. Then I went to the Cabinet Office to meet the Premier of Bermuda, Hon Jennifer Smith. I invited her to The Tattoo and to 'take the salute' in August.

The performance rehearsal went well, the Military Band in their smart scarlet uniforms and white helmets and the Gombey Dancers in flamboyant colourful costumes. I had suggested a steel pan player, albeit more West Indian, which gave a subtle atmosphere and started the performance brilliantly.

On my last day, I was invited to the exclusive Coral Beach Club by Major Giles Plowden, ex-Royal Scots Greys, and his wife. The Club overlooks the spectacular turquoise sea and the renowned and stunning pink beaches of Bermuda, a paradise indeed, and a perfect conclusion to a long trip.

The 2003 show was a great success. It was sold out and featured some new acts:

Bermuda Regiment and Gombey Dancers
Royal Army Band and *Pipes and Drums* From Oman.
Traditional Band From South Korea Never seen before in Europe.
The return of the awesome *US Army Drill Team*.
And to everyone's surprise and joy, the *Top Secret Drum Corps*
   from Basel.

As described in a previous chapter, we found this unique drumming group at The Royal Nova Scotia Tattoo and it was kept 'Top Secret' as it had never been seen before in Britain. The Drum Corps comprises young volunteers who are in business or at university and are dedicated to the cause, rehearsing three times per week. They are a hugely talented, dynamic, fast-moving Drum Corps with slick, precision drumming, stick throwing, and dress in Swiss traditional costume. It brought the house down!

Thus, we witnessed the birth of a top Tattoo act and following The Tattoo in Edinburgh, Top Secret was greatly in demand at Tattoos and events worldwide. Probably their most memorable moment, however, was appearing before HM The Queen at Windsor at three Jubilee Pageants – the Diamond Jubilee, her 90th birthday and the Platinum Jubilee.

They also appeared as a surprise at an autumn reception at Windsor Castle when all the players met Her Majesty.

Top Secret was the inspiration of Erik Julliard, a drummer from birth, who, following this extraordinary success in Edinburgh, gave up his career as a lawyer and later ran his own show in Switzerland, The Basel Tattoo. At the time, I said it was a mad idea, but The Edinburgh Tattoo would help in every way possible. The Basel Tattoo is now world-renowned as the second largest Tattoo after Edinburgh and has been hugely successful entertaining 100,000 per year. At the time of writing, it is in its seventeenth year.

CHAPTER 10
2004

SINCE THE COLLAPSE OF Soviet Russia, the end of the Cold War and the unification of East and West Germany in 1990, the three Services, the Army, Royal Navy and RAF have been considerably reduced in size by MOD 'Options for Change', endless cuts and redundancies. For example, reductions in the Army included all its Regimental Military Bands, around 30 of them which was a huge loss and deeply felt as they were the very heartbeat of many regiments and battalions. At the time of writing, little is left apart from the talented Bands of The Household Division and about five Staff Bands. The Bands of The Royal Marines and RAF, however, were sensibly left largely untouched.

Regimental Pipes and Drums continue to survive but the pipers and drummers are soldiers first so they have an operational role and are always busy.

The Tattoo, historically founded by the Army, has naturally been mainly Army-oriented and run. The other two Services, in my view, have not been included enough in this great international show. So, I decided to offer each Service a single Service year.

In 2004, it was the turn of the RAF. They could not have been more helpful:

RAF Massed Bands Four bands.
RAF Pipes and Drums They would muster two bands in their new specially-designed RAF tartan and join the *Massed Pipes and Drums*
The Queen's Colour Squadron RAF Ceremonial Unit and continuity drill.

And flypasts for the first time.
Potentially we had a great show coming together.
I now felt somewhat under pressure to bring in the other bands and acts for the programme. I had to specifically visit South Africa to meet

the South African Navy Band and see them perform; the People's Liberation Army Band, China, had never performed in Britain before and contact had not been easy so I had to urgently determine if they were committed or not – as they were key to my programme. I also had important meetings in Sydney regarding The Tattoo 'Down Under', which was imminent, and I had plans to visit some exciting new countries.

I was met at Cape Town by the Director of Music, Commander Mike Oldham, South African Navy. We had an initial discussion in my hotel, the excellent *Hotel Table Bay* with a stunning position between Table Mountain and the appropriately named Table Bay.

The next day, I was collected for a visit to meet the Navy Band at the South African Navy Base in Simon's Town (originally an important British Royal Navy base on the famous Cape of Good Hope). Interestingly, in those days it had the largest dry dock outside Britain, built for an expanding Royal Navy by British engineers with Portland Cement from home and granite blocks from Norway. It was opened in 1910, was crucial in two world wars and was handed over to South Africa in the 1950s. It is often used as an unusual open-air and below-ground auditorium for concerts. Whatever its usage, it remains an amazing work of art.

As we set off for Simon's Town, Mike Oldham said that before we saw the band we were going to meet a dog, an important dog. I immediately thought, *'Why on earth is he taking me to meet a dog?'* Simon's Town is a small, picturesque town by the Naval dockyard and in the town square, by the sea, is a bronze statue of a Great Dane. I was then told the fascinating story of this renowned Great Dane called 'Just Nuisance'.

During the Second World War, the Royal Navy were permanently using the Naval Dock at Simon's Town and a Great Dane living with his owner in the town, used to befriend the sailors who were on a run ashore and who fed him snacks and would take him for walks. He would also accompany the ratings to the pubs and lead them back to the ship when they were the worse for wear.

He would even go by train to Cape Town with them and became a regular traveller. Eventually, when he was in danger of being put down by the locals as they considered him a real nuisance, the Royal Navy stepped in and officially enlisted him, promoting him to Able Seaman which gave him full protection as a member of the Armed Forces!

He was renowned across the Royal Navy over those wartime years and when Just Nuisance fell ill, signals were sent to all Royal Navy ships telling them not to worry as he was bedded down in the Naval Hospital and was well cared for, but, sadly, he later died. Appropriately, he was buried with full military honours in the Forces' graveyard after which the statue was erected in his honour.

If only he had been alive, I would have invited him to The Tattoo. Eventually, we got to see the Navy Band.

I was most impressed by this unique brass and woodwind Military Band. Following the ending of Apartheid, the rules for the three armed Services required that they should draw 70 per cent from the Black community including Zulu and Xhosa, 20 per cent from the Cape Coloureds and those with Asian background and 10 per cent from the white population. Albeit somewhat complicated, this meant a rich mix of cultural talent and variety in the music to be played including the great anthem '*Nkosi Sikelel iAfrika*'. Mike Oldham and I had a long discussion on music and what would appeal in Edinburgh.

Following a fascinating morning, I was introduced to the Flag Officer Simon's Town, Rear Admiral Louw, and invited to lunch in the beautiful old *Admiralty House* situated by the beach. He was fully in support of my plans and helped with the band's official travel to Edinburgh. Following lunch, we visited the dry dock of which they were very proud. Later that day, I was invited to the annual Navy Garden Party, another old tradition – I was asked to address the guests about The Tattoo! I imagine that Simon's Town must have been one of the best Royal Navy postings in the British Empire.

That evening, for the first time, I met Pipe Major Charles Canning of the Cape Town Highlanders (affiliated to the Gordon Highlanders). They are an excellent band which, in later years, played many times in Edinburgh, at other Tattoos and even Windsor for The Queen's Diamond Jubilee.

Later on, I gave dinner to the Commanding Officer, a few other officers and Charles Canning of the Cape Town Highlanders in a rather good seafood restaurant by the old port. Having ordered drinks and dinner, I visited the loo around the corner from our table, en route I noticed Sean Connery and his wife, Micheline, sitting at a table. I had met him several times as he was a frequent attender and supporter of The Tattoo in

Edinburgh. On the way back, our eyes met and he invited me to sit down and asked, 'What on earth are you doing here?' There followed a long conversation. Meanwhile, my guests were wondering where I had got to and then noticed that I was sitting with no less than James Bond, so they were not a little impressed.

I was delighted with the South African Navy Band and the bonus of the Cape Town Highlanders Drums and Pipes.

I had to return to China to check on the results of my previous visit where serious progress had been made. But, as I suspected, the friendly Director of Music who I met on my last visit, who gave me that memorable lunch and was rude to the commissars, was nowhere to be found. Indeed, everything we had achieved on the previous visit had been forgotten, so my visit was opportune.

I was disappointed but we started again and heard the new PLA Band play, which was excellent and, through the interpreter, we discussed the music.

I bravely told the PLA colonels that we would prefer them not to wear the (boring) green PLA Army uniform. Had they a full dress? To my surprise, they asked what I wanted, so I said a red tunic, a red forage cap (for communist China) and white trousers. And that is how they arrived in Edinburgh. The good news, albeit they were unprepared, was that they had a green light from the top and were planning to come. The only thing we could not identify was if we would get a cultural act. This remained a mystery. Nonetheless, my mission was mainly successful.

On my return to Scotland, I received a telephone call from the head of the Free Tibet Movement who somehow had heard that China might be attending The Tattoo.

To my surprise, he said, 'I hear that you are inviting PLA China to attend The Tattoo.'

I replied, 'I never divulge the cast until July.'

He answered, 'If you do, you will have us to contend with.'

'Do I take that as a threat?' I questioned.

He was not overly friendly and I had never been approached like that before, which made me even more determined. Sure enough, we had plenty of trouble from the Free Tibet Movement and Falun Gong in August. More of which later.

CHAPTER 10 - 2004

A visit to Sydney was crucial as we had to tie up all the plans for the massive event in 2005 with the challenge of laying on the biggest Tattoo in the history of The Royal Edinburgh Military Tattoo and Australia.

The good news was that the Chief of Defence Force Australia, General Cosgrove, AC, MC (he was later appointed Governor of Australia), had given his full support for the event and the Australian Forces would therefore offer us:

> Their *Military Bands* and their *Pipes and Drums*.
> The *Federation Guard*, and an *Arena Party* as well as accommodation, transport, administration staff as necessary.

This was a big relief as without his support it would not have been possible.

The visit took the form of production and administration meetings as well as a press conference as there was huge media interest and meeting some of the key staff including, Colonel Patrick Pickett, the Australian Army Senior Director of Music, to discuss the musical programme.

We had to put the rest of the programme together by inviting our top acts and this was in hand. I also met with my friend, the President of Pipes and Drums Australia, Greg Gordon. He agreed to bring me another six Pipes and Drums which, including the Aussie Army and our regiments, would give us fifteen bands.

Regarding the vital subject of music, I felt during a previous visit that I was somewhat ignorant of Australian music so I went to their Piccadilly – Pitt Street – to find a music shop. There were plenty but the general response was, 'Australian music? We don't have any of that Mate'. I eventually found some CDs, mainly Aboriginal cultural, but there was one which I bought and took home. It had some appealing Aussie tunes including their great national anthem, 'Advance Australia Fair'. The one that I settled on was 'I am, we are, you are Australian'. I thought it would work perfectly with Pipes and had it arranged by the very talented Lieutenant Colonel David Price, OBE, my musical adviser. The Australian Army Senior Director of Music, Lieutenant Colonel Patrick Picket, looked at me very suspiciously but reluctantly agreed to go with it.

All was looking good so I was off across the Tasman Sea briefly to firm up the New Zealand acts and bands for the next two years, before flying 6,000 miles from Auckland across the South Pacific on an 11-hour flight to Chile, my first visit there.

I arrived at Santiago Airport feeling somewhat jaded. I had been travelling for days so jet lag was catching up perhaps.

The Defence Attaché, Colonel Iain Campbell, met me with his Land Rover Discovery and he said, 'You must be a bit tired after your long journeys so you have a choice, I take you to your hotel for a rest or would you like lunch in the Andes?' It was an easy decision. We went for the Andes and what a great experience, a delicious lunch outside, just below the impressive snow-capped Andes range (the highest in South America at around 22,000 ft).

On the way back, to add some Chilean atmosphere to the day, we visited the rodeo and by the time I found my hotel, the *San Christoph Tower*, I was ready for bed.

The subsequent day, I was invited to the equivalent of The Royal Military Academy Sandhurst and witnessed the Cadet Passing Out Parade which was slick and impressive. The culmination of the parade was when the cadets that were passing out were presented with their bayonets. I observed the Academy Band – smart as mustard who appeared to play well. They have an impressive full dress uniform of a powder blue tunic and pickle helmet with a red plume. This interesting uniform and tradition came from their close association with the Prussian/German Army before the Great War. Their drill and marching were also similar and included the high step (known to us as the goose step). I thought that this would go down well in Edinburgh.

I was introduced to the Chief of the Army and his staff – everyone was keen for a band to perform in Edinburgh. I followed this up with another visit.

On my free day, I was rather hoping to relax, but a trip had been organised to Valparaiso the main port of Chile and historically fashionable and important. I wondered why I was being taken to Valparaiso as there was plenty to see in Santiago which was closer. My guide was a British Army captain attached to the Embassy, Matthew Baker. On arrival, my guide said that we were visiting the Chile Navy Museum, but the penny still did not drop. As we entered the main door to this huge museum, on the right is a massive portrait of Admiral Lord Cochrane, the

10th Earl of Dundonald. Originally with the Royal Navy, he fought gallantly and successfully through the Napoleonic Wars. After leaving the Navy, 'under a cloud', he ended up fighting for Chile and became 'The Saviour of Chile', defeating the Spaniards and freeing up Chile as an independent state. So, I had the honour of meeting the acknowledged 'Hero of Chile', greatly feted and remembered. Yet another successful Scot.

Meanwhile, back in Edinburgh, The 2004 Tattoo was, thankfully, sold out with a great and varied cast. In the lead was the RAF with a huge contingent of four bands and the very professional Queen's Colour Squadron renowned for their perfection in silent drill. We had the flypasts of one or two fast jets every night in sync with the opening fanfare. Their top singer, Corporal Matthew Little, sang brilliantly in the finale. He later became a talented RAF Director of Music.

This was another remarkable moment in this show. I had asked the RAF for a violinist/fiddler for a finale number but they were unavailable. I had witnessed my eighteen-year-old goddaughter play her violin with great skill at two very painful family funerals – for her mother and her sister – cool, calm and collected. Subsequently, in consultation with her father, Major Hamish Macrae, ex-Royal Scots Dragoon Guards, I extended an invitation. I realised that this was a risk, as putting a young amateur on stage with professionals and a huge audience is a daunting prospect. If they fail, the individual will never forget the ignominy of it all, but if they succeed, it is a huge confidence booster and forever a triumph.

Our violinist was Rowena Macrae and rehearsals were very challenging and testing for her with 500 musicians, pipers and bandsmen as a backing group. She played the solo for 'Millennium Prayer' in the finale, looking stunning in a long tartan skirt, in front of the Combined Bands for 25 performances, 8,600 people per night, attended by a total of 220,000, without fault. It was indeed a triumph for her, and for the godfather and producer – huge admiration and a great relief.

The new acts that year were:

The excellent *South African Navy Band* playing jazz, rock, gospel and African songs, and marimbas playing 'The Lion Sleeps Tonight'.
Cheraw The bamboo dance by young people from Mizoram we had discovered some years previous.

Club Pirouette A rhythmic young woman's gymnastics act from Estonia. *People's Liberation Army, China* A military band initially delayed and held back for a general's inspection. They eventually appeared in the red hat and tunic as requested and the mystery cultural act turned out to be a very well-drilled tall women's group with PLA flags.

Our big problem that year was half expected with the presence of the Free Tibet Movement with whom we had sympathy. That said, we did not expect them to be 'in the face' and so very offensive, attempting to cause chaos daily: blocking roads with demonstrations when Edinburgh is in festival mode and at its most hectic; daily demonstrating at the entrance to The Tattoo office. I was quite busy with the show, then I was asked by the head of the demonstration to see the chief Tibetan monk so, showing willing, I invited him into my office with an interpreter. He spent two hours telling me, in Tibetan, about the problem with China.

The climax to this saga was when the Police Special Branch informed us that some tickets had been acquired by the Free Tibet Movement for the final BBC TV Night. We were given their names so we could easily locate their position in the stands and the Police suggested that we arrange to provide them with some tickets around them, just in case.

On the night in question, as the PLA Band marched into the arena, the Free Tibet people rose to their feet in demonstration mode with flags, banners and noise. What they did not know was that they were surrounded by the Police in civilian clothes who promptly arrested them. The demonstrations petered out after that incident and thankfully normality was restored.

After the show was over, BBC World informed us that China TV Channel 1 had bought The Edinburgh Tattoo's BBC production and it was viewed by around 200 million Chinese viewers. This was a classic example of The Tattoo's 'soft power' at work.

CHAPTER 11
2005

THE YEAR 2005 was the busiest ever, with the addition of our Tattoo in Sydney in January. It was, for me and the team, our biggest challenge. We had to ensure that The Tattoo at home was unaffected and as good as ever while organising and producing probably the largest military musical event since the Second World War – and, just to complicate things, it was 10,000 miles away *Down Under*!

The Tattoo programme at home looked promising with the first Royal Navy year – a celebration of the Senior Service and the 200th Anniversary of the Battle of Trafalgar. It was to feature an excellent cast including the Massed Bands of The Royal Marines, the Massed Pipes and Drums which included all the Scottish Infantry Regiments, sadly for the last time, as The Royal Regiment of Scotland was about to be formed (2006). In addition, we looked forward to a display by The Royal Marine Commandos, a Guard of Honour from The Royal Navy Reserve and some other brilliant acts.

But it was January so we were off to Sydney for The Edinburgh Military Tattoo Australia 2005.

There were two parts to our programme: Canberra for the evening ceremony 'Australia Day Tribute' and then Sydney for The Tattoo 'Salute to Australia'.

The former event was our opportunity to pay our respects at the Australian War Memorial and show British appreciation and thanks to our Australian cousins and those who served with the three Services through two world wars.

A contingent from the large Tattoo cast had been selected for this special event and flown in advance to Canberra. We arrived on 25 January, the day before Australia Day, and went straight from the aeroplane into heavy rehearsal mode, which was difficult and demanding as people were tired. It did not go at all well and when we performed our dress rehearsal at the Memorial, the Massed Bands for some reason were out of sync; it was chaotic as the arena was oval.

We decided to rehearse early the next morning when everyone was rested and the arena was squared off – our last chance to get it right. Two retired Australian generals were delighted to see the Brits having difficulty and were heard to say, 'Do they not teach drill anymore in the British Army?'

It was a disappointing and worrying start but the early morning rehearsal on Australia Day was excellent and the show ideal for the occasion – phew!

Later that morning, Steve Walsh, my Production Manager, and I were asked to the Australia Day ceremony near the lake under the gum trees.

The Federation Guard marched on to parade and then, to our surprise, the Prime Minister, John Howard, mounted the podium just yards away. During the ceremony, he addressed the parade and the people of Australia through Channel 1 ABC TV. It was such a good address; I even remember his main two points:

If you are an immigrant and new to Australia you are very welcome but please support our cricket and rugby team.

To all the volunteers across Australia, thank you for the large contributions you make to our country. We could not survive without you.

I liked the latter statement as no one ever thanks our volunteers at home.

After the parade, we were invited for a 'bite of lunch'. We expected a stand-up affair with sandwiches, but we were ushered into a large marquee and there was a seating plan. This was not a 'bite of lunch' it was a banquet. I was placed on the right of the Prime Minister with the Chief of Defence Force, General Cosgrove on the other. A fascinating lunch, it was a pleasure talking to John Howard which was a real privilege and the General and I had plenty to discuss about the Army, but I could not help thinking of the evening as we had a small show to run and were supposedly the stars of Australia Day.

After lunch, Steve Walsh, who was at a different table said to me, 'Clearly you had a good lunch and you banged on a lot about The Tattoo.'

'How did you know?' I said.

'You must have been sitting on your telephone as it was on permanent *send* throughout lunch and I could hear everything,' he responded.

The evening was balmy, sunny and warm – just perfect. The hierarchy had turned out: the Prime Minister with all his Ministers, the Chief of Defence Force and his staff from the three Services, Our High Commissioner, Sir Alastair, Lady Goodlad and Sir Alistair's team, the Lord Mayor, the great and the good from Canberra seated in the VIP stands and many friends, as well as 25,000 people ensconced on the grass banks around the Memorial and the arena. The Governor General of Australia, Major General Michael Jeffrey, AC, AO, CVO, MC, was asked to 'Take the Salute'. *No pressure then.*

This amazing war memorial looks down Anzac Parade to the Australian Parliament a mile away. Anzac Parade, wide and impressive, is Canberra's Mall or Champs-Élysées and runs down to the large City Lake called Burley Griffin.

The cast for this event comprised:

Massed Pipes and Drums of the Scottish Regiments – The King's Own Scottish Borderers, Highlanders, Argyll and Sutherland Highlanders and the Gurkha Rifles
Queen's Colour Squadron RAF
The Military Bands of The Royal Marines, Scots Guards and the RAF

On the hour, the Massed Bands marched up Anzac Parade to 'Combined Marches', 'Bonnie Dundee', 'The Atholl Highlanders' and 'The Glendaruel Highlanders'. It was a stunning sight with uniforms and accoutrements glinting in the evening sunshine, what a spectacle.

On arrival at the arena, the set piece ceremony included:

Massed Pipes and Drums
Queen's Colour Squadron Silent Drill Display
Military Bands
And a finale, which included the evening hymn, lone piper and national anthems

All went perfectly and just as well as expectations were understandably high from the top team in Australia.

Then, as is traditional, the Officer on Parade, OC Queen's Colour

Squadron, marched forward to the Salute Taker and asked, 'Sir, may I have your leave to march off the British Contingent – Sir, please?'

Normally the VIP would say, *'Thank you. Carry on please'* but General Jeffreys said, *'No you may not. I want to say a few words.'*

He went on to give the British contingent a huge accolade and ended by saying, 'Ladies and gentlemen let us all give our British cousins our thanks and a proper Australian welcome.'

The entire crowd rose to their feet roaring with applause for two or three minutes until the Governor eventually said, 'Thank you, please carry on.'

As the contingent marched into the sunset, I have to say that I was deeply moved, extremely proud and much relieved. The success of this important evening ceremony celebrating Australia Day was due to the skill and professionalism of our Directors of Music, Pipe Majors, our talented Pipers and Bandsmen and, needless to say, my Production Manager, Steve Walsh.

To round off the evening and Australia Day, our generous High Commissioner gave a formal dinner.

The large cast for the Australian Tattoo assembled in Sydney on 29 January 2005, mainly accommodated in the Sydney University Halls which was excellent, while the stadium, as planned, was the Aussie Stadium alongside the hallowed ground of the Sydney Cricket Ground Trust. The Aussie Stadium, famous as the main rugby arena, was now prepared for The Tattoo with an impressive lifelike Edinburgh Castle backdrop. It usually had a 45,000 capacity but with the backdrop could seat 27,000.

Leo Schofield had selected the renowned Sydney Cricket Ground Trust to organise and promote the event, an excellent choice and, in accordance with our wishes, it was a charity. By the time we arrived in Sydney, the show was completely sold out – 162,000 people were about to descend on us.

We would have just three days practice then a full dress rehearsal for the general public, followed by six days of performances.

After the first day's rehearsal – it had been a long day and fairly chaotic – I held a production meeting at around midnight. There were sound problems in that huge auditorium and the choir, the Massed Bands, electrics and soloists were way out of sync. The Senior Director of Music, from the Australian Army, was not happy and said at the meeting, 'Well that was b... chaos, I had expected better from the Edinburgh Tattoo – I want to know what the hell are you going to do about it with just two days to go?'

They all looked at me somewhat shellshocked by the outburst.

I said, 'Let us remember that this is just day one of rehearsals, and like our rehearsals in Edinburgh, it is the normal chaos of day one and tomorrow, believe me, it will all come together.'

I was concerned, but that is why we have rehearsals and indeed experts.

The next day, John Del Nero, our Tattoo sound designer, quickly sorted the sound so it was all on track; Steve Walsh worked miracles with the cast on the arena and it all started to come together. By the end of day two, we had a stunning show emerging from the confusion of day one with great music directed by our Senior Director of Music, Major Andrew Chatburn of the Irish Guards, including:

Probably the biggest, most powerful performance of 'Waltzing Matilda' ever witnessed, was played by the 300-strong *Military Bands.*

Combined Military and Pipe Bands Playing 'Hector The Hero'.

What went down best of all was 'I am Australian,' which featured vocalists from the *Australian Services* who were simply brilliant.

Without a doubt, we had a fantastic cast:

The Military Bands of *The Royal Marines, Scots Guards, RAF, and the Royal Australian Navy, Army and Air Force* Around 300.

Royal Scots Dragoon Guards, Royal Highland Fusiliers, King's Own Scottish Borderers, Argyll and Sutherland Highlanders, Royal Gurkha Rifles, RAF and the Lothian and Borders Police Pipes and Drums from home.

Royal Australia Regiment, Australia Reserve, Federation Tattoo, Queensland Police, Tasmania Police, Scots College and *The Royal Caledonian Society of South Australia* Pipes and Drums from Australia – altogether a total of about 300.

Queen's Colour Squadron RAF

The top acts were:

HM King's Guard From Norway.
New Zealand Army Band
New South Wales Mounted Police and Police Bands
Top Secret Drum Corps
OzScot Highland Dancers With Edinburgh Tattoo Dancers –
200 in total.
Federation Guard of Australia
Sydney Public Schools Choir
An *Aboriginal Act* with didgeridoos started the show.
A total of 1,500 performers.

Although we were told that it never rains in January, during the final rehearsal day we were warned of bad weather coming our way. I felt that we would work through it as time was short. It was being tracked by the hour then the minute.

The stadium team kept telling us, 'It's 30 minutes away, then fifteen minutes, then two minutes. Had you better not do something?'

As you would expect, we continued in true British fashion. It hit us with such force: torrential rain and storm-force winds, a classic severe Australian summer storm. The cast scattered for cover. Fortuitously, it was a rehearsal and not a public performance.

The six performances, however, went like a dream. The weather was perfect, the cast did so well and even in that huge auditorium, the Massed Bands were awesome. Our audiences loved the show.

We made a serious error on one night, however, with our High Commissioner taking the salute. We had two 40 m flags, the Union Flag and the Australian Flag – the dancers brought them out in two huge bags and unravelled them in the finale on queue. We unveiled the massive Australian Flag during their anthem 'Advance Australia Fair', which went perfectly but then as we were starting the British national anthem, the Union Flag, which had not been put away properly the night before, was pulled out by the dancers and appeared like a huge bow tie. Oh no! Nevertheless, the Australian audience loved it. I had to offer The British High Commissioner, however, my sincere apologies.

I asked various friends who lived in Australia, our cousins Ian Walker-Munro and his family, Scotchi and Pepi Walker, and Simon Dewar from home in Perthshire and brother of Lord Forteviot, to the show. He lived in the outback on his cattle ranch miles from anywhere. He said he was coming and then took me to lunch at the world-famous *Doyle's on the Beach*, which started as a hut on the beach in 1895 and was now a major seafood emporium. We had a great lunch of, yes, fish and chips. That night he and his wife, Sandra, attended The Tattoo.

The day after, I was invited to go sailing on a yacht in Sydney Bay with some friends who live in New South Wales. The owner and skipper with a large gin and tonic in one hand and steering the yacht under full sail with his foot, said, 'I hear you had Dewar at the show last night.'

I said, 'Yes, it was great to see them.'

He went on to say, 'That is some achievement as Dewar hasn't left his property for twenty years.'

We brought the main production team from Edinburgh including:

Production Manager Steve Walsh.
Tattoo Director and Lighting Designer Lieutenant Colonel Richard Hambleton.
Sound Designer John Del Nero.
Narrator Colonel Alasdair Hutton.
Senior Director of Music Major Chatburn, Irish Guards.
Director Army Bagpipe Music Major Stuart Samson.
Dance Director Billy Forsyth.
Musical Adviser Lieutenant Colonel David Price.

It was with great relief and huge satisfaction that the show appeared to be a huge success. The cast had a well-deserved day off before returning home.

That morning after the last performance, the Sydney Cricket Ground Trust informed me that I had been made an honorary life member, a privilege indeed. Then I was invited with some of the team to report to Sydney Harbour for a treat – another welcome cruise in Sydney Harbour. On arrival at the pier, this amazing gin palace/motor yacht appeared, coming astern towards us. We were ushered aboard and offered a glass of champagne, a nice mid-morning surprise. Apparently, they had asked the team what my favourite food was. They said 'fish and chips', so what did they give us for lunch? Lobster and fries – a special treat. We cruised around the Sydney Harbour past the famous Opera House and Sydney Bridge. It was a memorable way to end this wonderful experience.

A month or two later when the accounts had been finalised, I was informed that after all expenses we had made a surplus of £1.5 million, a record for The Tattoo. Our 50 per cent share went to our charitable company for Service charities and the Arts, and as part of our agreement with the Australian Forces, I flew back to Canberra to present General Peter Cosgrove, the Chief of Defence Force, with a cheque for £750,000 for his Service charities. I think it is fair to say he was not just surprised but stunned.

After a short break at home, we had a Tattoo to run in Edinburgh.

As it was the Royal Navy year, they turned out in force in celebration of the 200th Anniversary of the Battle of Trafalgar:

Three Royal Marine Military Bands
A Royal Marine Commando Display
Royal Navy Guard of Honour

We had a very strong cast:

The biggest *Massed Pipes and Drums* ever with thirteen bands.
The Trinidad and Tobago Defence Force Steel Band
A return of the ever-popular *Honda Imps Motorcycle Display Team*.
For the first time, the talented and brilliant *Russian State Cossack Dance Ensemble*.
And *The King's Guard, Norway*, who were celebrating their 100th Anniversary.

(Earlier in the year, I was invited to make an address at the 100th celebration in Oslo in the presence of HM King Harald. A high point on a tour of the Norwegian Resistance Museum was meeting the acclaimed 90-year-old Head of the Resistance in the Second World War, a modest and gentle man.)

As it was such a special year with the 200th Anniversary of Trafalgar, I decided that we must introduce some new technology to the show. 'Projection' was relatively new and unknown then but I had seen it that year with Sir Michael Parker from the Royal Tournament. We used it sparingly to start with as it has a really powerful effect on the production. The image that will forever remain in my mind is the stern of HMS *Victory* emblazoned on the Castle. The designer, Ross Ashton, cleverly lined up *Victory's* guns with the Castle cannon fitting perfectly to her port side, and we fired the Castle cannon as well. The last part of the vignette was Admiral Nelson being shot by a French sailor in the rigging of a French battleship. Nelson, one of Britain's all-time heroes, died as we know in the arms of Hardy but what did he really say?

People think it was 'Kiss me, Hardy,' but it was 'Hardy, I do hope that I have done my duty,' probably the greatest understatement of all time.

The narrator, Alasdair, ended the vignette with the following words:

'And ladies and gentlemen, the Royal Navy then ruled the waves for a hundred years.'

With the three Royal Marine Bands playing great naval music in the formation '200' and a superb finale with the white ensign and the Union Flag powerfully projected across the Castle, it was a memorable moment.

I made a difficult decision after the 2005 show. With eleven wonderful years as CEO and producer, I thought, sadly, that I really ought to step down at the end of 2006 and spend more time at home as I had been away so much. It would give someone else the opportunity to take the helm with new ideas, and as my wife, Sarah, said, 'Go when you're on a high.' So, I gave my notice to leave after the 2006 show.

CHAPTER 12
2006

THIS BEING MY LAST YEAR, clearly, my aim was to make The Royal Edinburgh Military Tattoo 2006 a really impressive one. The box office informed me that we were sold out at the end of January, with some 220,000 seats. This was extremely pleasing and indeed a record.

The plan for the year was an Army lead; two of their finest Military Bands, The Coldstream Guards and The Scots Guards, joined by the new band of the Royal Regiment of Scotland and our wonderful Gurkha Band. A huge Massed Pipes and Drums of thirteen bands, including the newly titled Pipe Bands from the Royal Regiment of Scotland, joined by our friends, the Cape Town Highlanders and the Queensland Police, two excellent Pipes and Drums.

The Highland Dancers, a vital part of any tattoo, deserve another special mention. We started in 1995 with just twenty dancers – all Scots in traditional mode – but now we were presenting a hundred every year with guest dancers from The Commonwealth – Australia, Canada, New Zealand and South Africa – impressively choreographed Massed Highland Dancing displays to great music. This proved to be a huge success at our Tattoos in Australia and New Zealand. Billy Forsyth, MBE, our Highland Dancing Director, was central to this success story and this new style of 'Massed Dancing' has now been emulated worldwide. Billy had many close contacts within The Commonwealth Highland Dancing Association. The best-known personalities who became great friends were:

> *Cheryl Roach* OzScot Australia who supported our Tattoo in Sydney with 200 dancers and performed frequently in Edinburgh and internationally.
> *Shirley Ann Thompson* From New Zealand. Her whole family danced and she also performed in Edinburgh and, of course, produced 200 for our Tattoo in Wellington.

In 2006, we welcomed 50 dancers from South Africa to join the

Scottish contingent. We also had some new acts and some scheduled for 2007 which I had to visit. This saw me make my first visit to Taiwan.

Due to the political tensions with China, I had to follow advice from the Foreign and Commonwealth Office to avoid an international incident. My visit was, as expected, extremely popular as Taiwan relishes recognition. Indeed, on arrival, I was met by a senior official in the Taiwan Ministry of Foreign Affairs with a large black limousine with flags. In the morning, I was summoned to a meeting with the Director General, British Trade and Cultural Office, which is a substitute for the British Embassy. I was advised not to invite the Taiwanese military, which might offend, so I began looking for a Taiwanese cultural group.

I was invited, however, to see the Taiwan Army Change Guard at the Chiang Kai-Shek Memorial Hall – emulating US Forces in combat uniforms, wearing chromium helmets and sunglasses – not the sort of uniforms we wore in the British Army.

They also took me to visit the rather scary Taipei 101, then the tallest building in the world at 1,667 ft, which they say is earthquake-proof.

I was informed about a youth group, 'The Taipei First Girls High School Band' so we had a meeting at 12 noon at the High School. It was a long session with the headmistress who went on a bit, so I asked boldly, 'Can we see the band and drums please?'

She replied in typical schoolmistress fashion, 'Patience, Brigadier, patience.'

We eventually went outside onto the massive square. I was astonished to see not just the band but around 500 girls in American college-type uniforms with miniskirts and boots, all standing like professional soldiers at attention with the Band and Drum Corps and a Guard of Honour in front. I was placed on a rather high plinth for the presentation of arms. To be saluted by 500 girls was a first for me. I acknowledged the Salute and I waited for something to happen. Eventually, the headmistress gave a signal and the parade swung into action.

They did very well. I witnessed impressive drills by these young people, with music and a slick Drum Corps. Albeit American in style and not Taiwanese, I thought being so young and so competent, they would go down well at The Tattoo so I booked them for 2007. I think they were thrilled and I was also pleased as the Taiwan Government was paying all the expenses for flying a hundred to Edinburgh.

CHAPTER 12 – 2006

From Taiwan, I flew via Hong Kong to China and Nanchang, a large city in Jiangxi Province, some 800 miles from Beijing in the middle of nowhere.

After the People's Liberation Army's visit to The Tattoo the previous year, I received an invitation from some Nanchang Tattoo organisers to visit. They had seen the People's Liberation Army perform at our Tattoo on Channel 1 China TV and wanted to start a Tattoo themselves in Nanchang.

So, as I was in Taiwan, which is close by, I thought I would accept the invitation and perhaps offer them a few ideas. As it turned out from the meeting at the airport, their agenda was far more than that – to milk me of all my knowledge during my short stay!

I was collected in a tiny Chinese car with my guide, Xie Jiangning, with a dodgy driver on a bumpy new motorway and the weather ice cold and wet. He started to question me straight away through a young female interpreter and recorded *everything* I said. I was beginning to think that this was not one of my best ideas. Even worse, I was then told that Nanchang was where the Chinese Civil War started, the birthplace of the People's Liberation Army and, in 1935, the start of the Long March of 5,600 miles which ended with the defeat of Chiang Kai-shek.

They dropped me at the hotel they had booked for me, the *Hotel Gloria Plaza*. There was nothing glorious about this place. It was the sort of hotel you want to avoid at all costs. I was relieved to find some friendly Americans in the lift.

I said, 'What are you doing here, business, I assume?'

'Oh no, we are here adopting babies,' they replied.

I could not believe it. This was also the children's adoption hotel and the lobby and restaurant were full of screaming newly found babies.

The next two days were pretty grim as they continued to interview me, a mix of meetings and trips to see the museum commemorating the Communist uprising, the highlight of which was the rather neglected Ming Temple, and all this was interspersed with generous lunches and dinners: normally fifteen courses.

Then I had an idea, there must be some Chinese culture to be found here, so at least The Tattoo gets some benefit from this visit. I asked the Nanchang Minister of Culture at dinner but he said there was nothing of note in Nanchang. (Nanchang seemed to be an enormous new city with empty skyscrapers everywhere.)

Disappointed, I said, 'Then what about Kung Fu?'

Their eyes lit up.

'Yes, there is a very good Kung Fu school just 60 km away.'

So, that was planned for my last day.

The Kung Fu school, Jiangxi Xishan International School, was 60 minutes away on another bitterly cold day. We arrived at the rather gracious gates of the school, almost ostentatious and certainly impressive. Sport was taking place on many playing fields. It felt just like a British Public School, a Chinese Gordonstoun perhaps?

I met the school's President. He informed me that the school looks after children from kindergarten to university age. I saw IT lessons, music, art, sport and the rest – masses of smart, uniformed and happy children.

I was then escorted to the gymnasium and sat on a solitary chair. Then, with the click of the master's finger, I witnessed a most professional action display from children aged seven to seventeen including martial arts, Kung Fu with swords and poles, and lots of jumping and tumbling. I was so impressed, that without further ado, I asked the headmaster if they could come to Edinburgh this year. He was very relaxed and agreed without reference to any commissars. I was told that airfares for 60 should not be a problem.

Accordingly, it was a successful afternoon. I asked my guide about this centre of excellence.

'I assume that it is free to all Chinese children,' I queried.

'Certainly not. It is a fee-paying school,' he replied.

I had discovered a private (what we call public) type school in communist China.

The last event on my final day was a traditional black tea ceremony back in Nanchang in a tea garden – fascinating small cups of delicious black tea (not the China tea we know), and I drank many cups as I was dying of thirst. So impressed was the tea supremo that he gave me a large chunk of black tea wrapped in newspaper – I would take it home.

Another fifteen-course banquet concluded the visit.

I am pleased to say that The Nanchang Tattoo started that year and is still running today with visiting bands from all over the world including Military Bands and Pipes and Drums from the British Army and the Black Watch Army Cadets.

I had also been invited to help in Brunei as the Army was planning a big show for the Sultan of Brunei, Hassanal Bolkiah, the absolute monarch and Prime Minister of Brunei since independence from Britain in 1984. It was his 60th birthday. The Sultan was educated at the Royal Military Academy Sandhurst and served briefly with the Irish Hussars, which was a great success. I agreed to visit and offer support for their big event. However, as I was flying into Hong Kong en route, I remembered the black tea wrapped in newspaper which looked rather suspicious. Knowing how strict Brunei is about drugs, I was somewhat concerned that I might end up in jail or at best delayed, so at Hong Kong Airport with which I was very familiar, I went to the old British Post Office and sent it back home in a brown envelope. Approaching Brunei, I read the landing/customs instructions which said in large print, anyone found to be carrying drugs would be executed!

I was met by two efficient Army majors and taken to the *Empire Hotel and Country Club*; a big 5-star hotel so big it took me fifteen minutes to get from my smart suite to the restaurant. At dinner, I realised that Brunei being Moslem was completely dry. This visit would again be good for my health.

I spent two intensive days running through everything with them: the production and all the related issues, the stadium and the backdrop – recommending projection to tell the Sultan's life story. We also discussed the massive administration and logistic effort. I think they were grateful.

On my last night, I was invited to dinner by a British officer, Lieutenant Colonel Ian Hamilton. He took me to the sailing club, which to my delight served wine – the only place on the island.

My next visit was to Singapore as I had heard so many good reports about their Police Bands.

I decided to have a treat and stay at *Raffles*, not only the best hotel in Singapore but famed around the world. It is named after Sir Stamford Raffles, a hugely successful British colonial officer, who founded Singapore and is credited with founding Britain's Far East empire. It certainly lived up to all expectations. It was stunning and I just had to try out the acclaimed Long Bar, renowned for its 'Singapore Sling'.

My visit was planned to meet and witness a display by:

Singapore Police Military Band A band of about 80. Their Directors of Music were trained at Kneller Hall, the *Royal School of Military Music in Britain*. An excellent sound.
Women Police Pipes and Drums Band A unique band.
Gurkha Pipes and Drums From the local Gurkha battalion employed mainly for security and a backup for the *Singapore Police Force* If necessary.
Cultural Dancers Extremely colourful.
This was a large well-rehearsed act of a hundred and perfect for The Tattoo so I invited them for 2007.

After the rehearsal, I was given lunch in the palatial pillared Police Officers' Mess, which before independence used to be the Officers' Mess of the Royal Artillery.

My rather hectic programme then included a brief visit to Australia to persuade the authorities to send an Australian Army Band to Edinburgh at some point as our association had become very close after The Tattoo in Sydney. It was a great opportunity to meet and thank all the old friends. Then I flew across the Tasman to Wellington once again, to persuade the Chief of Army to confirm that his ever-popular New Zealand Army Band would attend the show this year and to discuss the music and act in detail.

The New Zealand Army Band deserves a special tribute. Since its first memorable appearance at The Tattoo in 2002 for HM The Queen's Golden Jubilee, they have been greatly in demand internationally. They have a special style of professional military music and precision drill and then sheer comedy with music – unique in the world of Military Bands. The New Zealand Army Band have delighted people with their performance and is much loved. They are now the only regular Military Band in New Zealand so they are somewhat busy at home as well.

The Chief of Army tended to be unhappy about releasing the band, understandably as they were busy and he could not understand its worldwide popularity. Indeed, he always used to blame me for its success!

The last leg of my trip was to South America so I flew from Auckland down to Santiago for a brief stopover to see the Chilean Army act booked for this year – once again a long flight of eleven hours. New Zealand Air was excellent but it is not famed for its cuisine. At dinner, they offered New Zealand Sauvignon Blanc which I dislike, so I asked for red wine and they offered me Argentinian Malbec, new to me and, in those days, certainly not much in evidence at home. It was so delicious, I think I drank them dry. We are now drinking Malbec at home.

In Santiago, I was invited to lunch at the sophisticated Officers' Club, much smarter than anything the British Army has. It has tennis courts, swimming pools and an excellent restaurant to which we were invited by the Senior Director of Music for the Army of Chile, Lieutenant Colonel Guillermo Opazo. He commands 33 regular Military Bands and 31 Fife and Drum Corps, so we were noticeably getting the best for Edinburgh – the Concert Band of Chile. It will play stirring music and then the band will advance down the esplanade to the High Step from its old nineteenth-century association with Prussia and Germany.

Included in the act were the Chile cultural group from the professional Evendart Artistic Company providing a traditional dance display and Polynesian dancing from its South Pacific territory, Easter Island.

In the afternoon, I was invited by our Defence Attaché, Ian Campbell, to the polo to see the Chilean Ladies playing the English Ladies, a most interesting contest indeed which Chile won. The English Ladies were managed by Lord Sam Vestey who became Master of The Horse to The Queen. He was very kind to me when I was involved with the Windsor events mentioned in the next chapter. I also met the British Ambassador, Howard Drake, and Ian Anderson, 1st Secretary to the British Embassy, whose son Ross, by chance, later joined The Royal Scots Dragoon Guards and as I write is second-in-command of the regiment.

After a quick flight across the beautiful snow-capped Andes, we were in Buenos Aires – for my first visit.

I was surprised to be met by an official representative and whisked through customs in two minutes to the VIP lounge, where I met the Defence Attaché, Captain Chris Hyldon, RN, who took me to my hotel, the *Loi Suites*.

That evening, as I was quite hungry, I set off to find a restaurant near my hotel. Being ignorant of Argentinian cuisine, I chose Italian, sat outside with my book eating pasta and thinking it would be a boring evening when suddenly the street erupted with music and a couple appeared and danced Tango up and down the street with such style. It was a welcome surprise creating a special and dramatic atmosphere – free cabaret.

For the next morning, we had a full programme, first to the MOD to meet the Director of Army Staff who was supportive of providing a contingent for Edinburgh. Next we had a formal visit to the oldest regiment in Argentina, the Regiment of Patricians (Patricios), a large regiment of many battalions, some of which we sadly fought against in the Falklands War (Guerra de Malvinas). In British terms, they would be similar to our Guards Regiments in London.

I was greeted at the Guardroom by the Commanding Officer, Colonel Marturet, who welcomed me with a very smart salute. He was accompanied by his Directors of Music.

We were escorted to a dais on the Regimental Square and with a signal from the Commanding Officer the Regimental Band display began. I witnessed a 60-strong Military Band in a smart uniform of black top hats with feather and blue tunics, white breeches, red Cummerbunds and long black boots; the uniform being historically influenced by the French. The display included some dancing by the soldiers and altogether was very impressive stuff and perfect for The Tattoo. I was able to say a big 'Thank you' through the interpreter.

I was then given coffee and taken to the museum, which was fascinating. All was well until I viewed the last cabinet dedicated to the Guerra de Malvinas. In the cabinet was a Parachute Regiment beret, a Scots Guard forage cap and a Royal Marine beret, so I looked with interest not knowing quite what to say.

The Commanding Officer, seeing my difficulty, said, 'Don't worry, Brigadier, we all know that [President] Galtieri was mad.'

On that note, we departed as firm friends. I was so impressed by this Argentine Military Band which demonstrated the highest standards.

If that was not remarkable enough, I was taken to the Argentine Cavalry equivalent of our Household Cavalry in London.

We arrived at the palatial barracks of the Regimiento de Granaderos a Caballo, known as the Granaderos. I was greeted by a magnificent Guard of Honour – dressed in blue, Lancer-type uniforms with the old, curved sabres – on the grand steps leading to the front door of the Officers' Mess.

Honoured indeed. The Commanding Officer, Colonel Marcelo Carlos Gutierrez, greeted me at the door and ushered me into the San Martin Room of the Officers' Mess for coffee.

San Martin features everywhere in Argentina: General Jose San Martin liberated Argentina from the Spanish in 1816 and he is their national hero.

I was ushered out onto a stage at the other private side of the mess to see a dismounted march past by the Granaderos Military Band of 40, dressed in their Lancer-type uniform. Then, after more coffee and a brief on the fascinating history of the regiment, we saw the spectacular Mounted Band march past at the trot – 40 grey horses and four black Drum Horses, a truly magnificent and memorable moment. I felt so lucky to have witnessed these splendid bands.

The Colonel invited me and the Defence Attaché for a drink with the officers in glorious sunshine, gin and tonic in the mess garden. After half an hour, rather than overstay my welcome, I said that I must take my leave. That was not allowed. The Defence Attaché and I were expected to stay for lunch, which was a most memorable Argentinian BBQ with several meat courses accompanied by fine Malbec red wine.

This visit to Argentina was undoubtedly one of my most unforgettable. It was a privilege to visit this impressive City and Argentina's finest regiments with their great bands and unique culture and I was offered such generous hospitality. It also brought home to me the obvious facts of life and how stupid it was that we had to go to war with these charming people, who for years have been very pro-British and whose country is the second home of Aberdeen Angus as well as being the mecca of Polo. All due to a daft president, Galtieri.

On my last day in Buenos Aires, I was given a guided tour of the city by Chris Hyldon and, in the evening, we had a proper Argentinian dinner with a spectacular Tango cabaret.

The 2006 Tattoo went extremely well, thankfully, but we did have a very talented cast with two of the best acts:

New Zealand Army Band
Top Secret Drum Corps
As well as the finest *Massed Pipes and Drums* and *Military Bands*.

New to the show were:

Watoto Children's Choir A young Ugandan orphan's choir, organised by a charity that sing mainly gospel music. The children are, in the main, orphaned due to AIDS. I had met them a year before at the Scottish Business lunch, and was so impressed by their singing, I booked them. Then, wondering how I could best employ a children's choir, I meanly gave them just three minutes and all they would sing was a single gospel number, 'House of the Lord'. However, when I heard them again in rehearsal, I realised that I had missed a trick and these small engaging African children would be ideal for my big orchestral finale number, 'Can You Feel the Love Tonight', from *The Lion King* with Combined Bands. Their performance was great and I thought it all went very well. It can still be found on YouTube.

Jiangxi Xishan International School Kung Fu A group that I met by chance in China produced a great performance. Sixty young people gave an exciting display of martial arts, not seen before on the esplanade of Edinburgh Castle.

Concert Band of the Army of Chile and Cultural Dancers This great Military Band, dressed in pickle helmets and powder blue uniforms gave a brilliant performance of military music and dance, the first ever from South America.

And some old friends:

Top Secret Drum Corps They were better than ever and captivated the huge audiences – a star act. As if this was not enough, Erik Julliard had just produced his first excellent Tattoo in Basel.

New Zealand Army Band The band, which I first found in Wellington in 2000 at our Tattoo 'Down Under', gave us another outstanding performance of Kiwi music, Haka and comedy.

On one of the last shows, there was a surprise farewell ceremony. Sarah, my wife, had been warned off and was present that night, very importantly, as her contribution to the success of The Tattoo was enormous; she had kept the 'Home Fires Burning' during all my extensive, international visits, hosted dinner parties twice a week during The Tattoo season, entertained the heads of cast at home every year – at our last lunch, we entertained more than 60 from the cast and, importantly, she was my 'arch-critic'.

On the night in question, just before the finale, we were summoned down to the Esplanade from my production box with some apprehension on my part. To my total surprise and delight there was Sean Connery, and in front of the international audience of 8,600, the Lord Provost of Edinburgh, Leslie Hinds, said a few words:

Sean, who knew me well from various visits to the show and drams together, although he was not expected to say anything, in true James Bond style, he grabbed the microphone, turned to the audience, made a short speech and concluded, 'Tonight we want to thank my friend, Brigadier Mel Jameson, the producer of this great Edinburgh Tattoo for his service over twelve years...'

There was a huge reaction from the crowds at seeing this famous Scot and I was just extremely honoured.

I was kindly presented with a bronze replica of Edinburgh Castle. It was so heavy it went from Sean to me and then to my young and athletic aide-de-camp from the regiment, Captain Richard MacLure, to carry.

So that was it. For me, it was the end of an era, and an extraordinary and hugely rewarding experience, bearing in mind that I had been ordered to do it in the first place! It was exciting, challenging and sometimes extremely alarming as my head was always 'above the parapet'. It was also deeply satisfying that as a charity we were raising money for such good causes: the three Service charities – the Royal Navy Benevolent Trust, the Army Benevolent Fund (ABF The Soldiers' Charity) and the Royal Airforce Benevolent Trust – as well as the Arts and The Edinburgh International Festival. During my first year, I think we managed a mere £30,000, but by 2006, we were contributing around half a million pounds to charity annually.

I feel greatly honoured and fortunate to have had the privilege of producing The Tattoo for twelve years and some 300 shows and my thanks go out to all those who gave their support to The Tattoo and the many who took part: those from the three Services, our great Military Bands, Pipes and Drums, our Highland Dancers and all those from home.

It was also a great pleasure meeting so many wonderful people from many countries in our great Commonwealth and elsewhere across the world on my extensive travels; their contribution to the success of The Royal Edinburgh Military Tattoo is simply immeasurable. Finally, I was so well supported by my small select, very competent, charming and passionate team. It was for me a particularly difficult and sad decision to leave.

CHAPTER 13
Post-Edinburgh

Having departed the office, I found that I could not retire yet. First, I was extremely honoured to be appointed by Her Majesty The Queen to be Lord-Lieutenant of Perth and Kinross which was a new and very different challenge that would keep me very busy. Then some exciting Tattoo opportunities presented themselves.

• • •

Kremlin Zoria

IN THE SPRING OF 2006, I was contacted by my friend, Vitaly Mironov, from Moscow, who had helped me over the years to bring all those wonderful Russian acts to Edinburgh, the Navy Band Moscow, the Moscow Conservatoire Band and the Cossack Dance Ensemble in particular. He asked me to help him produce a Tattoo on Moscow's Red Square.

I told him, 'You must be mad,' knowing the complications and challenges of running a Tattoo let alone one in Moscow.

Nonetheless, I could not resist it and so I became co-producer of the Moscow Red Square Military Tattoo, *Kremlin Zoria*, which took place in September 2007 with the agreement of the Kremlin.

I had first to go to Moscow for a production meeting. I knew Moscow well by then but this was no ordinary visit. I was accommodated in a suite in the *Grand Metropol Hotel* situated beside Red Square, which was built just before the 1917 Revolution and is renowned for its Art Nouveau interior and, more recently, the best-selling novel, *A Gentleman in Moscow*. On my first day, I was invited to a parade by the Kremlin Guard inside the Kremlin – the 'Holy of Holies'.

I appeared as agreed at the heavily-guarded main gate where Vitaly and my friend, Dr Dmitry Fedosov, escorted me into the Kremlin and the central area beside the four great cathedrals where a crowd of Russian military officers – serving and retired – were gathered smartly dressed in modern uniforms and old Soviet uniforms, all heavily bemedaled.

We then waited in a stand for the parade to begin. In Russia, a stand is not a place where you sit as we do in Britain, in Russia, you stand! I noticed that, strangely, I appeared to be the only foreigner present. There were no ambassadors or Western guests.

I then witnessed the Presidential Regiment, the Kremlin Guard, the elite troops of the President, 'get on parade'. For me, being very familiar with British Army parades, this was fascinating. Appearing smartly in good military order I saw:

An Infantry Battalion of the Presidential Regiment Since 1990, for parades and guards, in addition to modern uniform, they are now dressed in the green/blue uniform based on the old Preobrazhensky's Life Guards with the double-headed eagle cap badge of the Tsars.
A Company of Spetsnaz The Russian equivalent of the SAS in their easily identifiable striped shirts.
Various Troops on BTR-60s The wheeled armoured car of the 1950s still in service.
A large troop of Mounted Household Cavalry of the Kremlin Guard Also in the Imperial uniform of 1914 based on Preobrazhensky's Life Guards, mounted on bay horses from the Kremlin Equestrian Centre.
The large Presidential Band of The Russian Federation Which played everyone onto parade to excellent martial music.

So that was impressive.

Then I noticed a tall, elegant officer parading up and down the various contingents. As he turned, he saw me and marched off parade in my direction, came to a halt in front of me, saluted smartly and said in perfect English, 'Welcome to Moscow.'

I learnt that this was Major General Valerie Khlebnikov, Commander of the Kremlin Guard, who had been briefed about my Tattoo involvement.

Next was the arrival of President Putin, greeted by Major General Khlebnikov, who then presented a large Standard to the Regiment. The Standard, modelled on the old Imperial style, was then trooped through the Kremlin Guard, with music from the Military Band to the cry from the soldiers of 'Hurrah, Hurrah, Hurrah'. President Putin then advanced towards us in the middle of the stands shaking hands with all the VIP contingent of guests.

Following the parade was a huge reception in the massive grand ballroom of the Kremlin Palace. A glittering 50 m long ballroom, with white walls and six massive stunning chandeliers down the centre. On the walls are the names, in gold, of those who died in Tsarist campaigns up to the Revolution. The reception was attended by VIPs and some of those on parade earlier, some 500 officers and soldiers, and there was vodka and plenty of it. I was then formally introduced to General Khlebnikov and his wife, Katherine. They were completely charming and welcoming, and later became good friends who visited The Tattoo in Edinburgh on several occasions.

That night, I returned to the *Grand Metropole Hotel*, and following a nightcap at the bar, I headed for the lift to my room. I could not help but notice, sitting on a sofa just by the lift, were five 'ladies of the night' with Scandinavian features. As I pressed the lift button, they smiled enticingly. Having avoided temptation, on arrival at my floor, two more appeared. I quickly locked the door.

The next morning, breakfast was particularly special as there was a harpist playing music on the stage, which, along with coffee, was a good way to start the day. I attended the production meeting where a most impressive programme was coming together: fourteen top Russian Military Bands with 800 Russian musicians. In addition, we would invite seventeen Pipes and Drums, 300 players from Britain and The Commonwealth. The groups already booked included two Russian dancing groups – Cossacks and Kuban Cossacks – The Royal Life Guards from Denmark, flag wavers from Italy and the Kremlin Presidential Drill Team and Cavalry Escort. Remembering the Great Patriotic War (Second World War) and 1812, they decided diplomatically to invite a German Military Band and a French Military Band – for a first-ever performance – and many other acts.

I was, as usual, concerned about the music, particularly for the finale, so I said to Vitaly that I must see the Senior Director of Music, who I had not yet met, to discuss the music for the finale. Most military directors of music that I had met were neither enthusiastic about performing with the Highland Bagpipes nor familiar with combined music. (Combined music is when all the Military Bands, made up of brass and woodwind instruments, join together with the Massed Pipes and Drums.) With so many bands involved – seventeen Pipes and Drums and fourteen Military Bands, it might be the biggest Combined Band ever so we did not want 'a cacophony'.

I set off in a black Staff Car to the other side of Moscow and into a grey and forbidding barracks. There, I was met by a soldier in jackboots who, without a word, escorted me up a grey stone staircase, and then in front of me was a double door. As the doors opened, there was a complete contrast from the gloomy barracks, a large, bright office with a grand piano, music playing and a pretty blonde on the sofa. I was very warmly welcomed by the renowned General Valery Khalilov, the Senior Director of Music for the Russian State Armed Forces, who was also a well-known classical conductor. He introduced me to his second-in-command, a colonel and saxophone player. He could not wait to let me hear his arrangements for the finale, which had been recorded earlier, and his second-in-command had learnt to play the pipes especially. The main pieces for the Pipes and Bands were 'Amazing Grace' (based on the original Fairbairn arrangement that I had sent), Russian folk tunes, 'The Banks of the Don' and what we know as 'The Carnival is Over', and other Russian music. We sat down and, as the music played, he looked at me apprehensively. Meanwhile, knowing how difficult it is to arrange combined music as the pipe chanter has a limited scale and plays in B flat only, I was not expecting this session to go easily.

However, I was completely astonished. Firstly, he had rearranged 'Amazing Grace' perfectly for the pipes and his Russian folk tunes, which were beautiful and emotional. The folk tunes were followed by some upbeat Russian music and then what better way to finish than the '1812 Overture' (without the Pipes) – the obvious choice for the 'Grand Finale'. Through the interpreter, I offered my sincere congratulations and a new friendship was made. We celebrated, of course, with a glass or two of vodka.

Months passed, and following The Royal Edinburgh Military Tattoo where I had just completed my handover to my successor, Major General Euan Loudon, I set off for Moscow again with some apprehension for the rehearsal week.

On the first morning, I saw the new stands erected for the show on the south end of Red Square in an L-shape with the vast Kremlin wall on the right, facing the most beautiful St Basil's Cathedral – what a backdrop! I also noted that the stands had been built over the top of Lenin's Tomb so there was not much reverence there.

The north end of Red Square was kept free for displays, which we witnessed later, by the awesome Cossack Mounted Display Team.

Thus, we were into rehearsals, emulating Edinburgh just three days before first-night, so it was, as ever, frenetic. I was most impressed with the quality of the acts. Powerful music from great Military Bands, outstanding dancing from the Cossack teams, precision silent drill from the Kremlin Guard and the well-trained Cavalry Escort. There was certainly plenty of talent.

On day one of rehearsals, General Khalilov found me and was desperate, as I was, to hear the Massed Military Bands and Pipes and Drums perform the combined music for the finale.

That afternoon, we heard them for the first time under the baton of Valerie Khalilov. The result was completely stunning: 300 Commonwealth pipers and drummers and 800 Russian musicians. Eleven hundred musicians in harmony providing a magnificent sound and a remarkable spectacle. This was going to be a great finale.

Rehearsals went well and for the first time in history, we had a Tattoo in Russia and in Red Square, with acts from all over the world. '*Soft power at work*,' I thought.

The first night was a huge success with a full house of Russians who had never seen a Tattoo before but gave an enthusiastic reception to the show. For the first time, they witnessed Massed Pipes and Drums, 300 players pouring out from Saviour Gate onto Red Square, a gate not used since Tsarist Russia. What a magnificent sight. Then, as predicted, the finale was superb – a great spectacle with this huge arena filled with colour and pageantry, many of the Russian Military Bands had discarded the Soviet-style uniform for the old Tsarist traditional full dress with the double-headed eagle emblem everywhere on the uniform.

General Khalilov mounted a huge dais and took command of 1,100 musicians and, with his arms stretched high, conducted with great skill.

To begin, we had 'Amazing Grace', starting with a solo from the Pipe Major of the Highlanders and, when the bands joined in, it was an awesome sound. One could hear the audience singing in the stands. Then, we had, unknown to us in the West, 'The Banks of The Don', a Russian folk tune – slow, emotional and incredibly moving. The audience applauded enthusiastically. After some more excellent music, the finale concluded with a three-minute extract from the '1812 Overture' with cannon firing from Spasskaya (Saviour) Tower and fireworks behind St Basil's Cathedral on which was projected images in glorious technicolour. On the last note of the Overture, Khalilov brought in the Massed Pipes and Drums and held it there. And that was another first!

Following the end of the show, we were invited to a reception in a large marquee behind the stands where the hierarchy gathered to celebrate a remarkable production. There was a ready supply of vodka, whisky, Georgian wine and even a liberal supply of caviar – a well-earned celebration for Vitally and the Russian team. A late night followed.

The next day, HRH Prince Michael of Kent was arriving. With the encouragement of my Russian colleagues, I invited him as he was such a good friend of Russia, a fluent Russian speaker and keen on Russian culture. We were in the Army together in Germany, he was in the 11th Hussars and I in The Scots Greys. We were honoured that he had agreed to take the Salute on night two and delighted that he was also staying in the *Grand Metropole*. The Russian producer, Vitaly Mironov, had arranged a formal dinner for him in the State Museum at the north end of Red Square. Prince Michael appeared in Royal Navy full evening dress with decorations and looked like Tsar Nicholas – uncanny! It was clear the hosts were not used to a royal Tattoo dinner, it took some time, as we had just finished the first course when it was time to leave for the show! It was, however, a great evening and I think he enjoyed it hugely.

We did not know there was another royal visitor present. Steve Walsh, my friend and the renowned Production Manager of The Royal Edinburgh Military Tattoo for twenty years, arrived at the bar of the *Metropole* and collapsed on the big sofa beside a young gentleman with glasses.

Thinking he was a member of The Tattoo team he nudged him on the arm and said, 'Who are you then?'

The young man replied, 'I am the Crown Prince of Denmark.'

He had come to see the Royal Danish Guard perform.

The next day, I was asked to entertain Prince Michael before his flight home as he was (I was told) my guest after all. There are two Italian bar-restaurants on Red Square: one cheap and informal and the other sophisticated with top-end cuisine. I planned to go to the cheap one for a relaxed light lunch. However, it was not to be as the other one had been booked, and worse, the party seemed to expand with 'hangers-on' including even the Russian security team. So we had a gastronomic lunch with fine Italian wine in Red Square's most expensive restaurant, the *Bosco Bar*. My American Express card melted as this, apparently, was my party.

Over the next few days, we were invited for a fascinating tour of the Kremlin Palace including the Grand State Rooms including the Hall of St George, the Grand Ballroom resplendent with chandeliers and the Hall of St Andrew, the throne room. St Andrew, as for Scotland, is the Patron Saint of Russia and the Order of St Andrew is the highest order of chivalry. Interestingly, they fly the St Andrew's Cross as a Navy flag on the stern of their warships but it is a dark blue cross on white, the reverse of Scotland's Saltire. We were shown the old private apartments used by the Tsars up to the mid-eighteenth century, which appeared rather small and basic. You can understand why they preferred St Petersburg as their home. In general, however, the Palace is very grand, hugely impressive and in excellent condition.

General Khlebnikov invited us to see a display by the Kremlin Equestrian Centre Cossack Display Team at the north end of Red Square. The Cossacks were the inspiration of the General and extremely talented. The Director of the Kremlin Equestrian Centre and leader of the Cossacks was Boris Petrov who later showed me his five-star stable complex. We witnessed a brilliant display of horsemanship.

A few years later in 2011, I recommended them to Major General Simon Brooks-Ward, Director of The Royal Windsor Horse Show, and they were invited to perform for HM The Queen at her Diamond Jubilee in 2012.

As the show drew to a close, the first Tattoo in Russia had been undoubtedly a huge success for Vitaly Mironov, indeed for us all, with a promise of a repeat in 2008. It was another example of 'soft power' at work and resulted in a strong bond of friendship, despite what I observed as a rather cold atmosphere at the political and diplomatic levels.

Sadly, circumstances rapidly changed in 2008. As The Tattoo was forming up in September, the Russian Federation invaded Georgia. On the Friday before the rehearsal week in Moscow, without any warning,

MOD London and HQ NATO sent an email ordering all NATO Bands to stay at home and not to attend The Tattoo 'Kremlin Zoria'. New Zealand was already in the air and the rest cancelled their flights. This resulted in Vitally Mironov's company going bust and the show's cancellation.

In 2009, albeit sad and annoying for Vitally Mironov, The Tattoo was taken over by the Kremlin knowing of its success. They renamed it Spasskaya Tower and successfully produced shows every year from 2009, most of which I attended.

Disaster struck in December 2016 when a military plane – a Tupolev TU-154 – carrying the Song and Dance Ensemble of the Russian Army, crashed into the Black Sea off Sochi. On board was General Valery Khalilov who sadly was one of the 92 killed. I sent a message to his family in Moscow – such a talented and charming man, a great loss for us all.

Despite the war in Ukraine, the 2024 Spasskaya Tower took place once again on Red Square and it was not surprising that the cast was made up of Russia's present friends – Belarus, China, the DPRK, Turkey, and, of course, the outstanding Russian bands, drill teams and dancers. It looked like a great show but, tragically, the Iron Curtain had descended again between Russia and the West.

• • •

The Basel Tattoo

MY OTHER EXCITING PROJECT was The Basel Tattoo, the story of which starts back in 2001 (as mentioned in a previous chapter). It is a remarkable story. Steve Walsh, the production manager, and I visited The Royal Nova Scotia Tattoo in Halifax, our sister Tattoo, produced by Colonel Ian Fraser (Former Canadian Black Watch) – an outstanding show that I visited every July.

During the 2001 Tattoo, we noticed a small drumming group at the back of the arena – very slick and hugely talented, throwing drumsticks at each other. We were so impressed that during the reception at the end of the show, I asked to see the group's manager. We were introduced to Erik Julliard, from Basel, the leader of the Drum Corps and I warmly congratulated him on the performance and invited him to our Tattoo. He said, 'Do you mean *The* Tattoo!' I suggested two years to build the act to around twenty as it was too small for us.

Fast forward to 2003. Unusually, I had not been to check this new act before the start of rehearsals – I must have had great confidence in them! So, it all came as a very nice surprise. On the first night, Top Secret emerged onto the arena sideways – a drumming group of twenty in a black, traditional Swiss costume, with side, tenor and bass drums, flying Swiss flags and offering extraordinary choreography. After an incredible display, they advanced down the esplanade and 'brought the house down'. It was a unique and simply stunning act – displaying precision drumming, slick drill and style; a top Tattoo act was born and the audience loved them.

In August 2003, I took Erik Julliard to lunch at our Tattoo restaurant, *Rusticana* in Cockburn Street, near our Tattoo office. Over lunch, Erik said, 'I have decided to organise a Tattoo in Basel – like Edinburgh.'

I said to him that I thought that was going to be really challenging, but we would help to get him started.

The first Basel Tattoo was in 2005 and took place in an ice hockey arena. I sent Steve Walsh to help as Production Manager. It was mid-July when Sarah and I visited Basel – very warm and humid. All went well but it was not a brilliant venue, so for the following year the watershed moment was changing venues to a new arena in the old Cavalry barracks in Basel by the great River Rhine – a good backdrop of two large towers and a central entrance to the arena, much the same size as Edinburgh. In 2006, The Basel Tattoo took off with a fantastic show entertaining around 120,000 people and had a great local following. It went from strength to strength and today it celebrates seventeen successful years.

The cast is always well looked after in Basel and are accommodated at local hotels within walking distance of the arena. Unique to The Basel Tattoo is 'the Cast Bar' with music and cabaret by The Tattoo acts, which is open all night, so the enthusiastic are there until the early hours, but back shipshape by the evening show!

Those more energetic would follow the old Basel tradition on hot days by jumping into the fast-flowing Rhine upriver then float down to the city centre where they would emerge, hopefully, alive and refreshed!

On leaving The Royal Edinburgh Military Tattoo in 2007, I was invited to be senior adviser to Basel, so from that moment I was honoured to be part of the team and this extremely successful show. I attended every year and travelled widely, most years with Erik Julliard, initially introducing him to a few of my international friends but always hunting for new acts. During these years, we visited Australia, China, Fiji, Tonga, Trinidad and Tobago, Hong Kong, Japan, Korea, Malaysia, Mexico, Oman, Russia and Singapore.

Erik Julliard is now renowned across The Tattoo world for his expertise and success as the Producer of The Basel Tattoo – everyone knows him, and he knows everyone.

Like Edinburgh, rehearsals were frenetic, running from 7 am to midnight daily. Sometimes, however, for lunch during rehearsal week, we would visit a remarkable restaurant called *Pica Bella* sitting on the balcony overlooking the Rhine and owned by the charming Christian Sidler. *Pica Bella's* normal menu comprised pizza, pasta, white wine, red wine and the finishing touch, grappa and espresso. Then back to rehearsals – all requiring significant stamina.

Basel was run on the same lines as Edinburgh with proper Massed Pipes and Drums from home and The Commonwealth, directed by the talented Captain Stuart Samson, ex-Director Army Bagpipe Music and Edinburgh Tattoo. We also had superb Massed International Military Bands conducted by the accomplished Swiss Army's Senior Director of Music and arranger, Major Christoph Walter. Over the years, Erik brought some new and brilliant acts to Basel and The Tattoo world including a wonderful Mexican Mariachi Band and cultural dancers, the world champion Blue Devils Drum and Bugle Corps from California, the Royal Cavalry from Oman and much more. Switzerland was represented by the much-loved Top Secret Drum Corps and the local, talented Swiss Army Bands; as well as the very popular troop of Swiss cows who came down from the mountains with their large traditional bells.

The Basel Tattoo is a triumph and a massive success story. It is now internationally regarded as one of the great Tattoos of the world, the biggest after Edinburgh. And from the cast's perspective, it is the most enjoyable and hugely popular.

• • •

The Royal Windsor Horse Show

ON RETIRING from The Royal Edinburgh Military Tattoo, I was invited by Major General Simon Brooks-Ward, director of The Royal Windsor Horse Show to assist with the production of a new Tattoo. This was to be held in the large arena situated in the private grounds of Windsor Great Park following the renowned Horse Show in the evening, an exciting prospect. The arena at Windsor is sizeable, built for horse events such as show jumping and dressage – we would need a large cast. Unlike most Tattoo arenas, this one was ideal for showing off the splendour of the horse: the great Mounted Bands of The Household Cavalry, the unique King's Troop Royal Horse Artillery, Musical Rides, Pony Club events and even Cavalry Charges. Horses were unsurprisingly the main theme for this Tattoo.

The Windsor Castle Royal Tattoo was directed by Simon Brooks-Ward and I was asked to be producer alongside the well-known Television Choreographer, Dougie Squires, as stage director. It successfully took place every year between 2008 and 2011 thanks to a great production team including Malcolm Wallace and the highly competent stewards/stage managers as well as experienced narrators like Alan Titchmarsh and Huw Edwards.

Throughout those years, in addition to great acts from home such as the Massed Pipes and Drums and Military Bands, we invited a huge variety of excellent talent from overseas, many of whom had performed at The Royal Edinburgh Military Tattoo, all old friends.

HM The Queen and most of the Royal Family attended from Windsor Castle on different nights with a suitable ceremonial arrival.

During those years, however, three really important events took place in that grand arena for Her Majesty The Queen and were televised by ITV. I was asked to assist as Consultant Producer and help find the many groups from abroad.

• • •

The Diamond Jubilee 2012

AN EXTRAORDINARY EVENT titled 'Around The World in 60 days' – a 90-minute show celebrating Her Majesty's Diamond Jubilee, her State visits to Commonwealth countries and her love of horses.

International Participants came from five continents. They included the Crème de la Crème of mounted contingents:

Zulus From South Africa.
Dancers From the Cook Islands.
Army Band From New Zealand.
Mariachi Band and Dancers From Mexico.
Cossack State Dance Company From Moscow, Russia

The Mounted Contingents:

Royal Cavalry From Oman.
Police Mounted Ride From New South Wales, Australia.
Mounties From Canada.
Huasos From Chile.
Dancing Marwaris Horses From India.
Cossack Mounted Display From Moscow, Russia.
Carabinieri Mounted Band Carousel From Italy.
Pignon Legendary horse whisperer from France with his loyal Greys.
Queen's Horses From Home.
Household Cavalry Mounted Musical Ride
King's Troop Royal Horse Artillery
Carriages and Horses From the Royal Mews.

What a show, what a cast and 600 horses. All memorable indeed!

• • •

The Queen's 90th Birthday Celebration 2016

THEN there was an even bigger show in 2016 to celebrate Her Majesty The Queen's 90th Birthday. It was held in the same arena with a cast of 1,500 from twelve nations and 900 horses.

This time we had a 'Global Village' on site where most of the cast were accommodated with 760 beds in 'bunkabins' and many caravans, a village shop and a massive marquee for meals and relaxing, and the post-show cast bar, which was an emulation of the one in Basel, providing music, dancing and cabaret from the cast. Somewhat surprisingly, Simon Brooks-Ward asked me to organise it and to start with I had to act as compère, which was certainly a new experience for me and there was not much sleep during that week. My reward, presented on the final night, was a sparkling Union Flag Jacket so you could see me coming a mile away!

Rehearsals are always frenetic and there was the day event, the Royal Windsor Horse Show, taking place as well. On one rehearsal day, we were informed that The Queen was visiting the arena and then I saw a green LR Discovery with The Queen driving. She stopped beside me so as the door opened, I greeted The Queen and bowed my head. I proceeded to present some of the team: the Atholl Highlanders commanded by the Duke of Atholl's eldest son, Michael, Marquis of Tullibardine, all the way from Blair Castle – they were thrilled – also the Cape Town Highlanders and Pipe Major Charles Canning, the Fiji Band and the New Zealand Army Band amongst others from The Commonwealth, who simply could not believe that they had met Her Majesty and quickly grabbed their mobile telephones to inform everyone back home.

After hectic days, somehow we arrived at the first night successfully. This time performers encompassed some of the foundations and pillars of The Queen's life including her love of horses and animals, the Armed Forces and The Commonwealth.

A summary of the programme is as follows:

Royal Arrival With Full Pomp and Ceremony Household Cavalry, Tri-Service Guard of Honour, the Band of The Irish Guards and the Queen's Body Guards (Gentlemen at Arms, Royal Company of Archers and The Knights of Windsor).

Mounted Displays By Shetland Pony Club Grand National, The King's Troop Royal Horse Artillery, Household Cavalry Mounted Musical Ride and the Royal Cavalry of Oman.

Vignettes of the Second World War and the Coronation.

International Salute By the Top Secret Drum Corps followed by the Azerbaijan dancers and horses and Chile Huasos.

The Commonwealth With the Fiji Military Band and Warriors, The New Zealand Army Band, the South Australia Police and the Mounties from Canada.

All The Queen's Animals Racehorses, mascots and drum horses; carriages and her favourite horses from the Royal Mews with her personal groom of 25 years, Terry Pendry, as well as polo ponies, and even Jersey cattle.

Braemar Gathering Vignette Including Massed Pipes and Drums and Aileen Robertson's Highland Dancers, the Atholl Highlanders and a big team from The Gathering.

All concluded with a massive finale under the Senior Director of Music, Lieutenant Colonel Nick Grace, RM, OBE, and with music throughout the show composed by the very talented Debbie Wiseman, MBE.

Later that year, in November, there was a reception held in Windsor Castle by The Queen to thank all the organisers and, unbeknown to her, the Top Secret Drum Corps appeared as a secret cabaret.

• • •

The Platinum Jubilee 2022

THE PLATINUM JUBILEE CELEBRATION took place on each evening of the Royal Windsor Horse Show in May 2022 and was one of the very few events that The Queen attended that year as she had reached the great age of 96 and was in delicate health.

A special lift was built into the Royal Box so that Her Majesty did not need to face the steep steps. Her Majesty arrived in the maroon Royal Range Rover with a full Household Cavalry escort and was greeted by a Tri-Service Guard of Honour and the national anthem.

This show was to be short and titled 'A Gallop Through History' – from 1588 and Queen Elizabeth 1 to 2022 and Queen Elizabeth II. It was indeed a gallop, but as in previous shows along with the theme, it was a

CHAPTER 13 - POST-EDINBURGH

display of the crème de la crème in equitation: rare horses from around the world, the finest Mounted Bands and ceremonial musical rides, the awesome King's Troop Royal Artillery and The Queen's much-loved horses and carriages from her own Royal Mews. Despite her infirmity, she was sitting forward in her seat fully concentrated on the action, occasionally laughing and, as ever, never 'missed a trick'.

This event saw equestrian performers and military acts from across the world pay tribute to The Queen and brought together a thousand performers and 500 horses over four nights. It was attended every night by different members of the Royal Family; the Sunday performance was attended by Her Majesty The Queen and broadcast live by ITV. It featured a raft of international personalities who took part in the show including Tom Cruise who introduced the Scottish act. Other stars included Dame Helen Mirren, Damian Lewis, Stephen Fry, Omid Djalili, Adjoa Andoh, Gregory Porter, Martin Clunes, Keala Settle, Alan Titchmarsh and Katherine Jenkins. The music was composed and conducted by the talented and renowned Debbie Wiseman, OBE.

The finale was short with announcements of thanks from Stephen Fry and Dame Helen Mirren who, dressed as Queen Elizabeth I, made the following statement:

> *Your Majesty many of us have played monarchs and have even played you. But none of us can comprehend how you carry the affairs of state with such dexterity and poise. I think I speak on behalf of us all when I say you have our thanks, our love and our devotion.*
>
> *For the past 70 years, you have carried the nation, you have been at its heart, you have been its drumbeat. You have unified us and given us purpose and when circumstances have been challenging, you have given us hope, guidance and leadership.*
>
> *To paraphrase Pope Sixtus's homage to Queen Elizabeth I: 'She is only a woman, only mistress of one nation and yet she is respected and adored across and by the World'.*
>
> *Your Majesty, our thanks are only matched by our loyalty to you in your 96th year and your 70th year on the throne of the United Kingdom.*

Following that powerful address, the Garrison Sergeant Major gave the order, 'Remove headdress', and three massive cheers to Her Majesty.

The Queen then left the Royal Box and departed in the Royal Range Rover with Her escort from The Household Cavalry as the cast and audience waved and cheered. This was, sadly, her final public appearance at the Royal Windsor Horse Show which she loved so much, and was one of her very last public events.

As Her Majesty departed, we all knew that this was 'the final one', so it was an emotional moment for us all, and for me, it was goodbye to the much-loved Colonel-in-Chief of my regiment (The Royal Scots Dragoon Guards), whom I had been lucky to meet on so many occasions.

APPENDIX

'Amazing Grace' by The Royal Scots Dragoon Guards

MY REGIMENT, The Royal Scots Greys, Scotland's senior and only cavalry regiment was amalgamated in June 1971 (as part of MOD defence cuts) to the 3rd Carabiniers to form The Royal Scots Dragoon Guards. We were at that time based at Redford Cavalry Barracks in Edinburgh.

Earlier in 1971, the new regimental combined bands, The Pipes and Drums, under Pipe Major Jimmy Pryde and Military Band under the Bandmaster from the 3rd Carabiniers, WO1 Herbert, joined together at Redford in preparation for the important Amalgamation Parade in July, which would be attended by our Colonel-in-Chief, HM The Queen and other members of The Royal Family. At that time, I was the Pipe President, and Major (later Major General) Charles Ramsay was Band President. However, he had been posted to Germany to command a Squadron of the 3rd Carabiniers for the run down to amalgamation. So, I was asked to look after The Military Band as acting Band President as well.

Earlier in Germany, we entered into a basic military recording contract with RCA Records, one of the leading recording companies in the world. We recorded two LPs with one to record as part of the contract. I was summoned to attend a meeting with the Commanding Officer of The Royal Scots Greys, Lieutenant Colonel Micky Blacklock. He correctly directed that this record should contain all the regimental music of the new regiment about to be formed – a good idea, RCA did not like! They would only agree to proceed if the Regiment would buy the first 1,000 records. Nor did they want the new names/regimental titles on the record as they were unknown to the public; so, as it was an old Scots Greys' contract, I decided on the title *Farewell to The Greys* with the subtitle *Welcome to The Royal Scots Dragoon Guards* and at last everyone seemed to be happy!

The record was not recorded in a smart Edinburgh recording studio, but in the study centre at Redford Barracks south of Edinburgh, with grey army blankets placed around the walls to improve the acoustics and it was completed with two 3-hour sessions in just one day.

As the last session neared the end, Pete Kerr, our record producer and friend, realised they were three minutes short on playing time, so an extra item was required. 'Amazing Grace', only recently arranged, was chosen, with Pipe Sergeant Tony Crease performing the solo piece. As recording time was running low, we were allowed just one take, and it was 'in the can'.

Why 'Amazing Grace?'

In 1970, Judy Collins produced a record of an American hymn called 'Amazing Grace' which became very popular. Indeed, it was a global hit but never quite reached the number 1 spot in Britain or USA. Of course, we all knew and loved the tune, but it was Pipe Sergeant Tony Crease who had the great inspiration to write an arrangement for bagpipes. He then asked our Bandmaster, WO1 Stuart Fairbairn Royal Scots Greys, if he would produce an arrangement for the Military Band to play along with the pipes. He did this over just two nights. I remember attending the first run of the arrangement in the barracks – it was a magical sound; great harmony, very special and loved by all who heard it at that time. So, it was for us in the bands an obvious choice to include on the recording, albeit RCA agreed rather reluctantly.

Following the recording, this new arrangement became increasingly popular at our performances in Scotland. However, the watershed moment was when Ian Fenner Producer of BBC 2's 'Late Night Extra Radio' programme, selected it from our LP, *Farewell to The Greys* – the disc jockey Keith Fordyce then played it once and over the next few days, the BBC received 30,000 letters enquiring about the record, so it was repeated the following week with even more letters. Ian Fenner realised that the track had commercial potential and tipped off RCA suggesting that it should be released as 'a single'. The RCA executives rather coyly admitted later that they were reluctant to take the decision seriously as it was military and bagpipes!

By the time it was released in March 1972, record shops had 30,000 advanced orders and continued to order quantities of 70,000 per day.

It soon sold 250,000 copies getting it into number 1 in the pop charts in just three weeks on 11 April 1972. I remember informing the commanding officer of our new regiment, The Royal Scots Dragoon

Guards about this great news that we were 'No 1 in the Pop Charts' – he said to me in his charming old-fashioned way, 'Mel I don't know what you are talking about – you handle it!'. So it was, I remember, bedlam as the press and media descended on the barracks for a press conference which I ran with the help of Pete Kerr, our producer, and the key player in this saga – by then, Pipe Major Tony Crease (later commissioned Major). We had some 100 attendees from the press and media, the BBC and STV included, and a surprised tam from RCA Records. RCA had informed me when we were all enthusing about 'Amazing Grace' at the time of the recording, 'Look, if we sell 5,000 copies of the album, we will be happy, and you will be happy'.

Following the press conference, the bands were summoned to the Top of the Pops Studio in London, a total of twenty in the Pipes and Drums and 35 in the Military Band – so 55 of us in full uniform arrived at the door of this renowned TV studio, in those days the 'Mecca' of pop music featuring iconic groups and singers such as The Beatles, The Rolling Stones and Donny Osmond– it was hallowed ground!

I was greeted at the entrance by a small man with long grey hair and a cigar. It was Jimmy Savile, who we all thought was rather strange. So, this was the first time military bands had performed at the Top of The Pops Studio and, on that day, they played live on the BBC 1 Top of the Pops weekly programme to an audience of around 15 million, cheered on by a mass of young fans!

The record remained at number 1 for six weeks selling a million records in Great Britain and then seven million worldwide earning eight Gold Discs from countries such as Australia, New Zealand, Canada, Germany, Japan and, of course, the UK where they received a Platinum Disc as well – *a legend was born*! The Pipers and Bandsmen were now pop stars and greatly in demand for UK tours, world tours and performances such as The Royal Variety Performance at the London Palladium in the presence of Her Majesty The Queen. 'Amazing Grace' finally sold thirteen million records, making it the biggest selling UK instrumental single of all time.

'Amazing Grace', however, was not universally popular. The Pipe Major and I were summoned to the office of The Director of Army Bagpipe Music at Edinburgh Castle and thoroughly reprimanded for demeaning the Highland bagpipes. Still, we pointed out to him politely that the sound of the pipes was being heard in a million homes in Britain and many more across The Commonwealth and the world.

Now 50 years on, the demand and enthusiasm for 'pure piping' and 'pibroch' today is certainly greater than ever, and globally has never been stronger amongst individuals as well as pipe bands. However, they all have 'Amazing Grace' in their repertoire!

'Amazing Grace' heralded a new style of music: the magical harmony of combined bands (pipes, brass and woodwind). This form of music became extremely popular and hugely in demand. Over the years, it has been emulated by Pipes and Drums and Military Bands at concerts and military tattoos in The Commonwealth and worldwide. And for The Royal Edinburgh Military Tattoo, combined music became the very 'hallmark' of the 'Grand Finale'.

TIPPERMUIR BOOKS

Tippermuir Books Ltd is an
independent publishing company
based in Perth, Scotland.

PUBLISHING HISTORY

Spanish Thermopylae (2009)
Battleground Perthshire (2009)
Perth: Street by Street (2012)
Born in Perthshire (2012)
In Spain with Orwell (2013)
Trust (2014)
Perth: As Others Saw Us (2014)
Love All (2015)
A Chocolate Soldier (2016)
The Early Photographers of Perthshire (2016)
Taking Detective Novels Seriously: The Collected Crime Reviews of
    Dorothy L Sayers (2017)
Walking with Ghosts (2017)
No Fair City: Dark Tales from Perth's Past (2017)
The Tale o the Wee Mowdie that wantit tae ken wha keeched on his heid (2017)
Hunters: Wee Stories from the Crescent: A Reminiscence of Perth's
    Hunter Crescent (2017)
A Little Book of Carol's (2018)
Flipstones (2018)
Perth: Scott's Fair City: The Fair Maid of Perth & Sir Walter Scott –
    A Celebration & Guided Tour (2018)
God, Hitler, and Lord Peter Wimsey: Selected Essays, Speeches and
    Articles by Dorothy L Sayers (2019)
Perth & Kinross: A Pocket Miscellany: A Companion for Visitors and Residents
    (2019)
The Piper of Tobruk: Pipe Major Robert Roy, MBE, DCM (2019)
The 'Gig Docter o Athole': Dr William Irvine &
    The Irvine Memorial Hospital (2019)
Afore the Highlands: The Jacobites in Perth, 1715-16 (2019)

'Where Sky and Summit Meet': Flight Over Perthshire –
A History: Tales of Pilots, Airfields, Aeronautical Feats, & War (2019)

Diverted Traffic (2020)

Authentic Democracy: An Ethical Justification of Anarchism (2020)

'If Rivers Could Sing': A Scottish River Wildlife Journey.
A Year in the Life of the River Devon as it flows through the Counties of Perthshire, Kinross-shire & Clackmannanshire (2020)

A Squatter o Bairnrhymes (2020)

In a Sma Room Songbook: From the Poems by William Soutar (2020)

The Nicht Afore Christmas: the much-loved yuletide tale in Scots (2020)

Ice Cold Blood (2021)

The Perth Riverside Nursery & Beyond: A Spirit of Enterprise and Improvement (2021)

Fatal Duty: Police Killers and Killer Cops: the Scottish Police Force 1812-1952 (2021)

The Shanter Legacy: The Search for the Grey Mare's Tail (2021)

'Dying to Live': The Story of Grant McIntyre, Covid's Sickest Patient (2021)

The Black Watch and the Great War (2021)

Beyond the Swelkie: A Collection of Poems & Writings to Mark the Centenary of George Mackay Brown (2021)

Sweet F.A. (2022)

A War of Two Halves (2022)

A Scottish Wildlife Odyssey (2022)

In the Shadow of Piper Alpha (2022)

Mind the Links: Golf Memories (2022)

Perthshire 101: A Poetic Gazetteer of the Big County (2022)

The Banes o the Turas: An Owersettin in Scots o the Poems bi Pino Mereu scrievit in Tribute tae Hamish Henderson (2022)

Walking the Antonine Wall: A Journey from East to West Scotland (2022)

The Japan Lights: On the Trail of the Scot Who Lit Up Japan's Coast (2022)

Fat Girl Best Friend: 'Claiming Our Space' – Plus Size Women in Film & Television (2023)

Wild Quest Britain: A Nature Journey of Discovery through England, Scotland & Wales – from Lizard Point to Dunnet Head (2023)

Guid Mornin! Guid Nicht! (2023)

Madainn Mhath! Oidhche Mhath! (2023)

Who's Aldo? (2023)

A History of Irish Republicanism in Dundee (c1840 to 1985) (2024)

The Stone of Destiny & The Scots (2024)

The Mysterious Case of the Stone of Destiny: A Scottish Historical Detective Whodunnit! (2024)

Salvage (2024)

A Most ~~Unsuitable~~ *Beautiful* Game: Celebrating Scottish Women's Football Fifty Years After the Ban (2024)

The Scottish Murder Book: Sensational Scottish Murder Trials. Book 1: Perth, Angus and Fife (2024)

William Soutar: Collected Works, Volume 1 Published Poetry (1923-1946) (2024)

William Soutar: Collected Works, Volume 2 Published Poetry (1948-2000) (2024)

The Road to Mons Graupius (2025)

'The Wheesht' The Best o Scots Hoose Yaldi (2025)

'The Perth Steamies': the Story of the Fair City's Public Washhouses, 1846-1976 (2025)

The Lass and the Quine (2025)

The Royal Edinburgh Military Tattoo: 'The Show Must Go On' – Travels of the Tattoo Producer (2025)

FORTHCOMING

'A Clear Divide': A History of Sectarianism in Scotland (Chris Bambery, 2025)

Disasters, Accidents & Enquirers in Scotland (Gillian Mawdsley, 2025)

Perth Academy: Its History (Gillian Dunbar and Alan MacDonald, 2025)

Many Lives! A Dundee GP's Memoir of the NHS at its Height (John Hulbert, 2025)

An Odious Campaign: How the 1936 Ross & Cromarty By-election Shaped British Politics (Ross McInroy, 2025)

William Sandeman (1722-1790): Perthshire Entrepreneur and Cotton Pioneer (Anthony Cooke, 2025)

Balkan Rhapsody (Maria Kassimova-Moisset, translated from the Bulgarian by Iliyana Nedkova, edited by Cara Blacklock and Paul S Philippou, 2025)

The Black Watch From the Crimean War to the Second Boer War (Derek Patrick and Fraser Brown (editors), 2025)

A Wildlife Guide to Edinburgh (Keith Broomfield, 2025)

William Soutar: Collected Works, Volume 3 (Miscellaneous & Unpublished Poetry) (Paul S Philippou (Editor-in-Chief) & Kirsteen McCue and Philippa Osmond-Williams (editors), 2027)

William Soutar: Collected Works, Volumes 4-6 (Prose Selections) (Paul S Philippou (Editor-in-Chief) & Kirsteen McCue and Philippa Osmond-Williams (editors), 2028+)

All Tippermuir Books titles are available from bookshops and online booksellers. They can also be purchased directly (with free postage & packing UK only; minimum charges for overseas delivery) from www.tippermuirbooks.co.uk

Tippermuir Books Ltd can be contacted at mail@tippermuirbooks.co.uk